The Mansion on Turtle Creek

THE MANSION ON TURTLE CREEK COOKBOOK

Haute Cuisine, Texas Style

ROSEWOOD MANSION ON TURTLE CREEK

with HELEN THOMPSON

foreword by DEAN FEARING

photography by ROBERT M. PEACOCK

RIZZOLI
NEW YORK

New York · Paris · London · Milan

First published in the United States of America in 2012
by Rizzoli International Publications, Inc.
300 Park Avenue South
New York, NY 10010
www.rizzoliusa.com

2012 2013 2014 2015 / 10 9 8 7 6 5 4 3 2 1

Helen Thompson was a food writer at *Texas Monthly* and an editor at *Metropolitan Home*.
Her articles have appeared in *Elle Décor, Men's Journal, Architectural Digest,
Traditional Home,* and *Veranda.*

Design and packaging by Janice Shay/Pinafore Press
Rosewood Production Manager: Stephanie Hutson
Rizzoli Project Editor: Christopher Steighner
Food/location styling: Denise Gee
Styling assistant: Rebecca Sherman
Primary tabletop source: Neiman Marcus
Source for several tabletop items: Dahlgren Duck
Additional photography, pp. 17, 18, courtesy *The Dallas Morning News*/Joe Laird

Printed in China

ISBN: 978-0-8478-3653-6
Library of Congress Control Number: 2011938453

Contents

Foreword

THE 1980S REPRESENTED A SHIFT IN DALLAS CUISINE, and the Mansion on Turtle Creek restaurant—where I served as chef for more than two decades—led the charge. When times are good, diners are open to new things, they're willing to experiment, and the Mansion was in a prime position to launch a daring and unproven culinary style—a new Southwestern cuisine.

At the Mansion there has always been an eye on culinary innovation. We were in the forefront of marrying French methods to the culinary traditions of Mexico and Texas. In a 1996 story titled "Texas Food Conquers the World," food writer Patricia Sharpe looked back on the genesis of this new cuisine: "Suppose you added a purée of ancho chiles to a classic demiglace? Why not take a corn husk and make a tamale of rice pudding with crème anglaise? The only possible answer to these questions was another question: Why not?" The Mansion restaurant was the perfect kitchen to experiment and perfect this new style of Texas cuisine.

I still remember the day Caroline Rose Hunt—the Mansion's founder—asked me to put tortilla soup on the menu. And I remember the uncertainty when we introduced the lobster taco in the restaurant: "Would people like it?" They did—hands down. You'll find recipes for both dishes in this book, and the Tortilla Soup remains just as popular today as when we first served it.

I have wonderful memories of the excitement generated by the menu we created and the celebrity list of guests that came to our table. I never knew who I would be cooking for on any given day—Mick Jagger or Elton John; Liza Minnelli or Frank Sinatra; the King of Spain or the King of Saudi Arabia; Margaret Thatcher or any of the, count 'em, last five American Presidents. The Mansion has and continues to entertain celebrities and dignitaries from the world over.

Another enduring memory: In 1985 the Mansion hosted the American Institute of Food and

Wine dinner to honor Julia Child, and we put together a menu that included whole catfish and blue-corn tamales. Though the Mansion waitstaff were more than slightly nervous about what they were serving this iconic figure of American cooking, there was no reason to worry. Julia loved all of it!

People are fascinated with intricate, exotic preparations, but they love familiar and comforting flavors. From those days as chef at the Mansion to the present, diners have enjoyed haute cuisine, Texas-style. When I compare the kind of food that comes out of the Mansion kitchen then and now, I see a common theme—the food is fresh, local, seasonal, and bold. It's a direct reflection of the people

of this city—worldly, modern, and ever evolving—and always true to our regional roots.

For 21 years the Mansion on Turtle Creek was my heart and soul—it's an icon of the best of Texas. I'm proud to be a part of the Mansion's tradition of excellence and I hope you enjoy these recipes from more than three decades of fine cuisine. *—Dean Fearing*

THE HIGH ART OF
TEXAS LUXURY CUISINE

THE ROSEWOOD MANSION ON TURTLE CREEK restaurant, bar, and hotel are steeped in the swank and swagger of Dallas history. Kings and queens, rock stars, presidents, athletes, and visitors from all over the world have wheeled up its circular drive and been whisked into the cloistered dining rooms of the 1920s Italianate villa. Locals who live in the posh neighborhood think of the Mansion as their private club. They are lured here by the reputation of the cuisine and a confident and intelligent menu.

At the Mansion a guest can dine on artichoke soup with Parmesan truffle fritters, seared scallops and fried sardine samosas, and braised pork cheeks with Texas-grown grits. Or, a gourmand can request a favorite dish and the chef will aim to please. An eccentric eater can even petition for a McDonald's hamburger (it has happened—a room service request presumably enjoyed behind closed doors). Someone from the Mansion's kitchen discreetly stepped around the corner to the nearby McDonald's and fetched the Quarter Pounder. "We will do anything to make our guests happy," observes Hugo Reynosa, restaurant captain since 1991. That generosity is the driving force behind this cookbook, which is the culmination of more than 30 years of imagination, dedication, and innovation. The recipes in this book are meant to be used and shared and, most of all, to expand your culinary world in exciting new ways.

For more than three decades, the restaurant and hotel housed in the peach-colored villa have set the standard in southern hospitality. At first glance, it's a standard by which luxury is defined. Only at second glance is it apparent that the standard isn't traditional in concept, in

execution, or in attitude. It stands alone—a sentinel of individuality and personal vision. There is one reason for the idiosyncratic interpretation of what luxury and service must be, and that reason is the Mansion's founder, Caroline Rose Hunt.

When Caroline Rose Hunt was growing up in Dallas in the 1930s, ideas of luxury and style were firm if not immutable. Hunt was on intimate speaking terms with both luxury and style. As the daughter of the spectacularly rich and nonconformist oilman H. L. Hunt, she traveled early and often through the United States and Europe—and the young lady took note of the implicit hallmarks that gilded the high life. She took note, and registered her disapproval: "When I was nine, we went by train to the New York World's Fair," she recalls. "We ate in the dining car, and the menus were in French, which nobody could read. I thought that was silly and couldn't understand why they weren't in English." Hunt never forgot her indignation, which was reinforced on a trip to Europe. Hunt was accustomed to the gregarious bonhomie that's distinctly Texan. It doesn't exist, though, east of the Red River—especially in Europe's finest hotels. "The staff in the European hotels were not friendly," she recalls.

Caroline Rose Hunt

At the time, Hunt had no reason to take remedial action, and the recollection of snooty service in restaurants and hotels became just a childhood memory. Never in the young girl's wildest dreams did she think that it would come in handy, much less that her notion of Texas-style luxury would form the bedrock philosophy for an entrepreneurial venture. For one thing, she says, "I never intended to be a hotelier." Beyond those early impressions of the hospitality enterprise, Hunt admits: "I knew nothing about the restaurant or hotel business." Except, it turns out, that what she did know would be all she needed.

Mrs. Hunt—as she is known both formally and affectionately—opened the Mansion in 1979. "My son Stephen had traveled in Europe, and he enjoyed the ambience of the smaller residential hotels. He thought we needed one in Dal-

The dining room of the Sheppard King mansion, now part of the Mansion Bar.

las." Mother and son didn't have to look far to find the ideal candidate. The Sheppard King mansion circumspectly faced Turtle Creek, the lush waterway that meanders through the heart of Highland Park, where many of Dallas's rich and famous dwell—and it was for sale. A bonus: This mansion already had an impressively strange pedigree that had guaranteed its legendary status in the annals of the city's madcap wealthy.

Originally built in 1908 by cotton baron Sheppard King, the palatial residence was destroyed by fire in 1923. Seizing the opportunity to improve on the original, the Kings trekked through Europe with their architect, J. Allen Boyle. Their goal was to procure luxe elements for a new house that elaborated on William Randolph Hearst's castle at San Simeon. The couple bought 19th-century Spanish cathedral doors, ornate grapevine-entwined columns, and Italian marble. Boyle designed an L-shaped mansion with a central spired cupola. The home's foyer featured a cantilevered staircase—considered a feat of engineering—that is still in place today. As is the

The original Spanish-style Sheppard King mansion, built in 1925.
Below, the library with its intricately carved fireplace by Swiss woodcarver Peter Mansbendel is still intact today.

oak-paneled library, with its carved plaster ceiling and richly ornamented stone fireplace surround, based on the parlor at Bromley Palace in England. The dining room, now the Mansion bar, has a ceiling inlaid with 2,400 pieces of wood, still intact today. The home had five bedrooms, four baths, and four maids' rooms—a total of 10,000 square feet, just enough space for the Kings to burnish their reputation for hosting lavish parties. But in 1935 the couple lost their fortune after the bottom fell out of the cotton market, and they were forced to sell their mansion. Oilman Freeman Burford and his wife, Carolyn Skelly (of the Skelly oil fortune), were first in line, with a $75,000 check and their own nearby house as a trade-in.

Under the Skelly-Burford reign, goings-on at the mansion continued nonstop: The couple hosted President Franklin Roosevelt, Louisiana governor Huey Long, and movie stars galore. Carolyn Skelly entertained herself by shopping obsessively and indulging in serial redecorating. Her excesses finally drove her husband to divorce her, and Carolyn was forced to fall back on the largesse of her ever-less-indulgent father. One by one, her servants decamped, and the heiress started selling off personal antiques as well as her own clothes. Finally, in the 1940s, the desperate doyenne rented out cottages on the property. Tennessee Williams was a visitor, and it was there that he wrote *Summer and Smoke*. At the end of the decade, oilman Toddie Lee Wynne purchased the estate for his American Liberty Oil Company's headquarters, and for the next 30 years daily life at the mansion was comparatively staid; nightlife there was nil.

But a new day dawned on the house with a past, when Caroline Rose Hunt bought it

The foyer featured marble floors, a cantilevered staircase, and carved columns. The staircase was such a feat of engineering that contractors from St. Louis, Kansas City, and Denver came to witness its construction.

Not far from the Mansion, the Mediterranean Spanish-style upscale shopping center Highland Park Village was built in 1931.

with the idea of opening a restaurant and hotel. During the two-year $21-million makeover, no cost was spared to bring the home back to its original resplendence. Hunt dreamed big for the restaurant, which was at first managed by New York's famous 21 Club. But Hunt staffed her restaurant with locals and had to look no further than the Pyramid Room at the downtown Fairmont Hotel to find her new executive sous chef. Dean Fearing was then an exuberant youngster, partial to crisp white chef's coats, blue jeans, and dramatic custom Lucchese cowboy boots, and in 1985 he became the chef at the Mansion on Turtle Creek.

Fearing, the son of a Kentucky innkeeper, had a goal: to become a great American chef. His methods were unorthodox, but the phenom was in the right place at the right time. Fearing's ascendancy at the Mansion paralleled the rise of a culinary movement fostered by Alice Waters, chef and owner of Chez Panisse in Berkeley, California. Waters's philosophy was inspired and simple: Cooking should be based on the finest and freshest seasonal ingredients produced sustainably and locally. Fearing agreed. He happened to be fascinated by regional food, and especially by Tex-Mex food, a beloved culinary cliché. Along with fellow chefs Stephan Pyles, Robert del Grande, and Ann Greer, Fearing focused on the might of fresh local ingredients and invigorated tired recipes with fresh ingredients like homegrown peppers, jicama, dried chiles, cilantro, and tomatillos, not to mention Texas Hill Country wild game, birds, and venison.

The Texas-based movement was dubbed New Southwestern Cuisine and soon captivated the rest of the country. Epicureans and groupies hung on Fearing's every creation in the Mansion's restaurant. Some dishes—notably the tortilla soup, now listed at the very top of the menu—are still available, even though Fearing has since moved on to his own eponymous restaurant in Dallas. Still firmly entrenched at the Mansion, though, is the commitment to local ingredients. If anything, the commitment is stronger than ever—you'll see in the pages of this book the people who grow the food served at the Mansion and you'll read their stories. And it will be obvious that great food is the result of personal dedication, from start to finish.

Under Fearing's jumpstart, awards for the restaurant began rolling in—and they have never stopped. The Mansion quickly became Dallas's darling, and it has remained so for more than three decades. The restaurant has always been a magnet for the rich and famous, and the list of legendary regulars is long. It includes Frank Sinatra, Elizabeth Taylor, Farrah Fawcett, Omar Sharif, Madonna, Francis Ford Coppola, Cindy Crawford, Richard Gere, and Bill Cosby ("He loves the tortilla soup," says Mrs. Hunt. "We make it for him whether he stays here or not"). Emmit Smith, Mark Wahlberg, and Mel Gibson check in too.

Inevitably, though, huge egos have meant that a certain amount of friction has agitated the usual tranquility at the Mansion. After a 1987 concert at Reunion Arena, Frank Sinatra marched in with some of the Rat Pack—including Sammy Davis, Jr., and Liza Minnelli—in tow. The Chairman of the Board insisted on seating the entire gang at a single table, although none was large enough. The Mansion staff improvised and pushed together two tables in the center of the room. Not so private for Sinatra, who was accused of rebuffing fans, but diners got a ringside view of the impromptu dinner party.

Things were simpler in the late eighties: Two decades later turf battles were between entourages, not individuals. A standoff occurred when Paul McCartney gave a Dallas concert and

Above, Caroline Hunt Schoellkopf; Above right: April 4, 1986, from left: Vivian Young, Robert Zimmer, and Caroline Hunt Schoellkopf; Above lower right: April 5, 1986, from left: Caroline Hunt Schoellkopf, Bunker Hunt, and Caroline Hunt

wanted the Mansion bar to himself and his friends afterward. So, too, did actor Nicholas Cage, also a guest at the hotel. Tension flared as each star's handlers asserted their primacy, but restaurant captain Hugo Reynosa stepped in with a solution worthy of King Solomon: "We settled the matter by converting the adjacent library to a temporary bar for Cage. Sir Paul and his group got to stay in the bar." The occasion was also memorable for Reynosa for another reason: "It was the first time I had ever heard of a martini with Red Bull, which was a favorite of Cage's. We had to go around the corner to a convenience store to buy the energy drink."

Royalty and heads of state also feel right at home at the Mansion. Princess Margaret, the queen of Thailand, the king of Sweden, G. H. W. Bush, George W. Bush, Jimmy Carter, Bill Clinton, and the crown prince Abdullah of Saudi Arabia have all made a night of it at the restaurant. Some, such as Saudi Arabia's crown prince, simply rented the entire hotel, thus ensuring a stay untroubled by the demands of other guests.

The environment at the Mansion that fostered Fearing's creativity more than three decades ago continues to thrive. Historically, offerings at the Mansion have ranged far and wide—from French to New Southwestern to pan-Asian with a Texas twang, and back again to haute Texas cuisine with a French flair when Bruno Davaillon joined the Mansion as executive chef in October 2009.

A native of the Loire Valley in France, Davaillon was raised on a farm and learned to appreciate fresh, local ingredients—a commitment he continues at the Mansion. His culinary interest was further sparked by Sunday dinners at his grandmother's house. Everything she served was fresh—she even churned her own butter. This was all very exciting to a young boy, and he began his formal culinary education at the age of fourteen. Davaillon gained early experience as the *premier commis* in two Paris Michelin-starred restaurants—Restaurant La Ligne and Restaurant Lasserre. He subsequently moved to London to work in the legendary three-star Michelin restaurant Tante Claire.

In 1997, Chef Bruno brought his talent to the United States as chef du cuisine at the St. Regis Los Angeles. Before joining the Mansion, he was executive chef at Mix, owned by the famed chef Alain Ducasse at the Mandalay Bay Hotel & Casino in Las Vegas. Under his five-year leadership, Mix was awarded Michelin stars in 2008 and 2009.

Chef Bruno has found himself right at home at the Mansion, part of the fellowship of the chefs who have preceded him—all have been in love with the many facets of American cuisine. He is the perfect chef to carry the Mansion's banner of culinary excellence into the future.

Always one to use ingredients from his own backyard, Chef Bruno is especially enthusiastic about local produce—tomatoes, melons, and peppers—and indigenous game, such as quail and venison. "I'm inspired by American culinary ingenuity, and Texans take that to a new level. I have applied my style and French technique to the Mansion menu, but when you dine in the restaurant you'll find the one thing that hasn't changed is the commitment to Texas flavors."

Texas is in a unique cultural position because a multitude of ethnicities settled the state. Germans, Mexicans, the French and Alsatian, African-Americans, and, lately, Asians, have flocked to the state. The food is a reflection of that serendipitous and convivial mix, and you'll find many recipes in this cookbook that reflect this.

The Mansion opened the door to a reconsideration of all cultural influences, far-flung as well as local. It's a luxury few restaurants dare to indulge. But at the Rosewood Mansion on Turtle Creek, high-spiritedness is appreciated. Here, it's the norm, a sophisticated paradigm of what luxury food should be but rarely is—except, that is, in Texas.

Enjoy dining with the Mansion,
Helen Thompson

Appetizers

Beef Sirloin Tartare

Red Snapper Ceviche

Arctic Char Confit

Grilled Gulf Prawns

Grilled Asparagus Risotto

Crispy Pork Belly

Lobster Cannelloni

Pan-Seared Crabcakes

Warm Lobster Tacos

Duck Confit Quesadillas

Potted Duck and Foie Gras

Beef Sirloin Tartare
with potato crisps and quail egg

SERVES 4

TARTARE
10 ounces lean Kobe beef, or prime
   sirloin, cut into 1/8-inch dice
2 tablespoons finely diced gherkins
2 tablespoons finely diced red onion
1 teaspoon chopped capers
2 tablespoons chopped chives
Sea salt and black pepper
1 teaspoon fresh lemon juice
1 tablespoon extra virgin olive oil

POTATO CRISPS
1 Idaho potato
4 cups peanut oil
Sea salt

QUAIL EGGS
4 quail eggs, yolks in their shells
Sea salt
Cracked black pepper

Combine the beef, gherkins, red onion, capers, and chives in a chilled mixing bowl. Cover the bowl with plastic wrap and refrigerate.

Peel the potato and slice it paper thin, lengthwise, on a Japanese mandoline, then cut into 3 x 1-inch strips. Reserve the slices in a bowl of cold water.

Heat the peanut oil to 340 degrees F in a 4-quart saucepan over medium heat. Drain the potatoes and pat them dry. Fry the potato strips in the hot oil in small batches, stirring with a slotted spoon to cook evenly, until they are golden brown on both sides. Drain the hot crisps on paper towels and sprinkle them with sea salt.

When ready to serve, remove the tartare from the refrigerator and season with a pinch of salt and black pepper. Toss the tartare in the fresh lemon juice and olive oil.

To serve, place a 4-inch ring mold in the center of a chilled, round dinner plate and fill the mold with a quarter of the tartare mixture, packing it slightly at the edges. Carefully lift the mold off and repeat with the remaining three portions. Place one quail egg yolk in a shell in the center of each tartare serving, season the yolk with a pinch of salt and black pepper, and garnish the plate with the potato crisps. Serve immediately.

Red Snapper Ceviche

SERVES 4

Combine the snapper and the lime juice in a large mixing bowl. Set the bowl in another bowl filled with ice, cover, and chill in the refrigerator for 1 hour.

After 1 hour, drain the snapper and discard the liquid. Add the red onion, fennel, cilantro, extra virgin olive oil, salt, and white pepper and toss to mix.

To make the sauce, combine the aji amarillo paste, kanzuri paste, garlic, ginger, vinegar, white soy sauce, lemon juice, yuzu juice, and sake in a blender and pulse until the mixture is smooth. With the blender running, drizzle in the grapeseed oil until it is fully incorporated.

To serve, spoon the red snapper mixture into four chilled, stemless martini glasses. Place the glasses in serving bowls filled with crushed ice. Drizzle 1 teaspoon of the sauce over each serving and garnish with the rice crackers and a sprig of cilantro.

8-ounce red snapper fillet, sliced into
   thin strips
Juice of 5 limes
1 small red onion, thinly sliced
½ bulb fennel, diced
2 tablespoons thinly sliced cilantro
3 tablespoons extra virgin olive oil
Pinch sea salt
Pinch cracked white pepper

AJI AMARILLO SAUCE
2 tablespoons plus 1 teaspoon aji
   amarillo paste (Peruvian product
   found in Latin markets)
½ teaspoon kanzuri paste (found in
   Asian markets)
3 cloves garlic, grated
1 tablespoon grated ginger
¼ cup rice vinegar
1 tablespoon plus 1 teaspoon
   white soy sauce
2 teaspoons fresh lemon juice
2 teaspoons yuzu juice (found in
   Asian markets)
2 tablespoons sake
2 tablespoons grapeseed oil

GARNISH
Japanese rice crackers for garnish
4 cilantro sprigs for garnish

Red snapper from the Gulf of Mexico makes this a fresh dish, perfect for summer. For parties, serve it over ice.

Arctic Char Confit *with American caviar*

SERVES 4

6 cups extra virgin olive oil
1 sprig thyme
2 bay leaves
1 tablespoon black peppercorns
½ tablespoon sea salt, plus more
 to taste
Black pepper
1-pound Arctic char fillet, skinless
 and deboned, cut into 4 equal
 portions
½ pound arugula, washed and dried
Zest and juice of 1 lemon
2 ounces white sturgeon
 American caviar

In a saucepan over low heat, heat the olive oil to 140 degrees F, using a thermometer to make sure to maintain the temperature. Add the thyme, bay leaves, black peppercorns, and ½ tablespoon sea salt. Cook for 10 minutes to flavor the oil with the aromatics.

Season the fish fillets with a pinch of salt and black pepper on each side and submerge the fillets in the hot oil. Cook for 12 minutes for medium-rare fish, or longer if you prefer well-done fish.

Toss the arugula with a drizzle of the cooking oil, a pinch of salt and pepper, and lemon zest to taste.

To serve, top the arugula salad with the fish fillets and add a generous spoonful of caviar and a drizzle of lemon juice to each fillet.

  The oiliness of the Arctic char works well, but you can substitute a nice Scottish salmon, if you prefer. Ask your butcher to remove the pin bones from the Arctic char for you.

Grilled Gulf Prawns
with watermelon and cucumber salsa

Combine the prawns, olive oil, garlic, lime juice and zest, chile powder, and cayenne pepper in a mixing bowl. Toss the ingredients together to coat the prawns. Season with salt and black pepper to taste. Cover the prawns and allow them to marinate in the refrigerator for 1 hour.

To assemble the salsa, place the cucumber, watermelon, red onion, jalapeño, lemon juice, and honey in a mixing bowl and toss to combine. Season with salt and pepper to taste. Add the olive oil, cilantro, and mint and toss to combine. Cover the salsa and let it marinate in the refrigerator for 30 minutes.

Cook the prawns on a hot grill for 3 minutes on each side. Serve on a platter with fresh cilantro leaves, lime wedges, and Watermelon and Cucumber Salsa on the side.

12 jumbo Gulf prawns, peeled and
   deveined, with the head on
¼ cup extra virgin olive oil
2 cloves garlic, crushed
Juice and zest of 5 limes
1 teaspoon ancho chile powder
½ teaspoon cayenne pepper
Salt and black pepper

**WATERMELON AND
CUCUMBER SALSA**
1 English cucumber, peeled, seeded,
   and cut into ¼-inch cubes
1 pound seedless watermelon, cut
   into ¼-inch cubes
1 red onion, minced
1 teaspoon minced jalapeño pepper
Juice of 2 lemons
1 tablespoon honey
Salt and black pepper
2 tablespoons extra virgin olive oil
1 cup chopped cilantro
½ cup chopped mint
Cilantro leaves
Lime wedges

 You will enjoy the sweetness of Gulf prawns.
Grill them with the head on for a better flavor.

Grilled Asparagus Risotto
with shiitake mushrooms

SERVES 4

2 medium shallots, minced
7 tablespoons unsalted butter
½ pound whole fresh shiitake
    mushrooms, stemmed
5 cups chicken stock
2 bundles pencil-sized asparagus,
    2-inch tips removed, stalks reserved
2 medium shallots, sliced
2 cups Arborio rice
1 cup chardonnay
½ cup grated Parmesan cheese
1 tablespoon mascarpone cheese
Salt
Freshly ground black pepper
¼ cup shaved Parmesan, for garnish
Extra virgin olive oil

In a sauté pan over medium heat, sauté half of the minced shallots in 1 tablespoon of the butter until the shallots are tender. Add the mushrooms and toss them with the shallots in the pan. When the pan becomes dry, add 2 tablespoons of the chicken stock and cook until the mushrooms are well caramelized. Set the mushrooms aside.

In a sauté pan over medium heat, sauté the asparagus tips with 1 tablespoon butter. Add 1 tablespoon chicken stock and continue to toss until the asparagus tips are bright green. Add the asparagus to the mushrooms and set aside.

Cut the reserved asparagus stalks into ⅛-inch rounds, taking care to only use the tender parts. In a sauté pan, sauté the sliced shallots with 1 tablespoon of butter until tender. Add the asparagus stalks and enough chicken stock to almost cover the shallots and asparagus in the pan. Cook, stirring occasionally, until the asparagus is al dente and bright green. Place the asparagus stalks in a blender and puree until smooth, adding reserved cooking liquid to the blender as needed to get the asparagus moving. Reserve the puree.

In a 4-quart, heavy-bottomed saucepan over medium-high heat, sauté the remaining minced shallots with 2 tablespoons of butter until tender. Add the rice and continue to stir for about 2 minutes. Add the white wine and stir constantly until the liquid has almost evaporated. Add enough chicken stock to barely cover the rice and continue to cook, stirring occasionally, until the chicken stock has been absorbed. Repeat this process several times, covering the rice with stock until the rice is mostly cooked and all the stock is absorbed. The rice should still have a little bite to it.

Reduce the heat by half and add the grated Parmesan, mascarpone, and ½ cup of the asparagus puree, stirring constantly until the rice is very creamy and fully cooked. Stir in 2 tablespoons of butter and a pinch of salt and black pepper.

To serve, spoon the hot risotto into four deep bowls and top with the warm sautéed asparagus and mushrooms. Garnish with shaved Parmesan and a drizzle of extra virgin olive oil.

The Source / AMERICAN HOMESTEAD NATURAL PORK

WHO CAN RESIST A PIG? Not Dee McLaughlin, if the pig is a Hampshire hog. McLaughlin—the owner of American Homestead Natural Pork—was in high school when he met his first Hampshire, a handsome domestic breed that's about as stylish as a pig can get. With its upright ears and glossy black body encircled around the middle by a band of white that extends down its front legs, the well-muscled pig proved irresistible to the Abilene, Texas, student: "I fell in love," McLaughlin admits.

The object of the future farmer's affection was worthy. Agriculturalists are crazy about the noble Hampshire for its sweet temper and good mothering traits. Chefs and culinary enthusiasts admire the pig for those reasons, too, although it's not immediately obvious why lovability makes for a fine pork chop. But Hampshire sows nurture their young, which encourages healthy piglets that thrive under the glow of maternal attention. Motherly love and good health bolster another Hampshire trait—the pigs are fast growers.

Dee McLaughlin's youthful admiration for the black and white import from Hampshire, England, proved prophetic: Hampshire pigs are best suited for a mission that McLaughlin decided to pursue after a career in the corporate meat industry. "I wanted to do something that was better for the consumer and that had quality

attributes." In 2005 McLaughlin started a new business, American Homestead Natural Pork: "We do nothing but all-natural pork," he says. "We don't use antibiotics or growth hormones; our animals receive an all-vegetable diet and are raised on family farms in unrestricted environments." McLaughlin knows his pigs personally because he's actually scanned hundreds of boars' backs with an ultrasound device that detects the highest marbling scores. Good marbling equals good taste, and the high-tech breeder can select pigs with the highest marbling quotients to sire progeny sure to produce succulent chops, lip-smacking ribs, robust roasts, sultry bacon and hams, and fork-tender tenderloins.

"I occupy a very specialized niche in the food industry," says the farmer. McLaughlin's customers include the Mansion, where American Homestead's flavorful pork products are deftly transformed. The crispy pork belly—sided with the elegant flavors and textures evoked by caramelized cabbage—is an evanescent reincarnation of the boneless cut of fatty meat from the belly of the pig. "It has the perfect balance of fat and meat," notes one of the Mansion's chefs. Diners with heartier appetites take particular delight in the braised pork chops with creamy grits, a graceful evocation of downhome Texas comfort food. The give and take of rich flavor with straightforward satisfaction is the reward.

Crispy Pork Belly *with Caramelized Cabbage*

SERVES 4

Combine 8 cups of water and all of the brine ingredients in a large stockpot and bring to a boil over high heat. Remove the pot from the heat and allow the brine to cool completely. Once the liquid is cool, submerge the pork belly in the brining liquid and refrigerate for 24 hours.

The next day, remove the pork belly from the brine and rinse the meat under cool water for 5 minutes. Dry the pork on a towel and discard the brining liquid.

Preheat the oven to 300 degrees F.

Heat the vegetable oil in a sauté pan until hot and cook the pork belly for 3 to 4 minutes on each side, or until it is a golden brown color. Transfer the pork to a cookie sheet and bake it in the oven for 1½ hours. Remove from the oven, slice the meat into ⅓-inch-thick slices while still hot, and set aside.

In a large sauté pan, heat the olive oil, garlic, and cumin seeds over high heat. Add the cabbage to the pan and cook, stirring often, for 10 minutes, or until the cabbage is lightly caramelized. Add the chicken stock to the pan, reduce the heat, and cover. Allow the mixture to simmer for 30 minutes, stirring frequently. Remove the cabbage from the heat and toss in the chopped scallions. Season with a pinch of salt and pepper to taste.

To serve, scoop the cabbage onto a deep plate and top it with hot slices of pork belly. Garnish with the chopped chives and shaved radishes.

BRINE LIQUID
¾ pound salt
Zest of ½ lemon
Zest of ½ orange
1 teaspoon coriander seeds, crushed
3 whole cloves garlic
1 bay leaf
3 juniper berries

2 pounds boneless, skinless pork belly
1 cup vegetable oil

CARAMELIZED CABBAGE
3 tablespoons olive oil
2 cloves garlic, minced
1 teaspoon cumin seeds
1 head (about 1½ pounds) green
    cabbage, cut into large cubes
2 cups chicken stock
1 bunch scallions, chopped
Salt and black pepper

1 tablespoon chopped chives, for
    garnish
1 bunch French breakfast radishes,
    thinly sliced, for garnish

Lobster Cannelloni
with butternut squash and Parmesan

SERVES 4

In a sauté pan over low heat, cook the bacon until almost crisp. Add the shallots and sauté until soft. Add the spinach, diced lobster meat, and tarragon and cook until the spinach is soft. Transfer to a bowl and refrigerate for 1 hour. When completely cool, stir in the ricotta and a pinch of salt and white pepper. Return the bowl to the refrigerator until you are ready to use.

Preheat the oven to 375 degrees F. Boil the cannelloni shells in generously salted water for 5 minutes. Cool in an ice bath and pat dry with a paper towel. Using a spoon, stuff the cannelloni shells with the lobster-spinach mixture. Place the shells in a baking dish and brush with extra virgin olive oil and sprinkle with the Parmesan cheese. Bake for 15 minutes. When warm, broil the stuffed shells briefly to brown the tops and remove them from the oven.

In a medium saucepan over low to medium heat, cook the butternut squash in 1 tablespoon of butter for 2 to 3 minutes, tossing frequently. Add the chicken stock and salt and pepper to taste and cook until tender, about 10 minutes.

In a sauté pan over medium heat, cook the lobster claws and tails in 1 tablespoon of butter for 5 minutes. Split the tails lengthwise and season with salt and pepper as desired.

To make the emulsion, heat the cream, half-and-half, and Parmesan over low heat in a saucepan until the Parmesan has melted. Pass the mixture through a conical strainer. Season with salt and agitate with an immersion blender until the mixture becomes foamy.

To serve, divide the squash among four large, shallow bowls. Top with the cannelloni and warm lobster claws and tails. Agitate the emulsion once again with a slotted spoon and spoon the foam around the dish. Garnish with the whole tarragon leaves.

2 ounces bacon, finely diced
2 shallots, minced
¾ cup baby spinach, washed and dried
6 ounces diced lobster meat, plus
    2 tails and 4 claws
1 tablespoon chopped tarragon, plus
    leaves reserved for garnish
2 ounces fresh ricotta
Salt
Cracked white pepper
8 cannelloni pasta shells
Extra virgin olive oil
¼ cup grated Parmesan cheese
2 cups peeled, seeded, and diced
    butternut squash
2 tablespoons unsalted butter
1 cup chicken stock

PARMESAN EMULSION
1½ cups heavy cream
½ cup half-and-half
1 cup grated Parmesan cheese
Salt

Pan-Seared Crabcakes
on jalapeño grits and sautéed greens

SERVES 4

To make the crabcakes, combine the crabmeat, onion, egg, scallions, lemon juice, bread crumbs, and parsley in a mixing bowl and toss to combine, being careful not to break up the crab pieces. Season the mixture with a pinch of salt and black pepper and the Tabasco. Divide the mixture into four portions, shape into cakes, and set aside.

Sauté the kale in 2 tablespoons of butter until wilted. Season with salt and black pepper and set aside.

To make the grits, combine the chicken stock, cream, and butter in a saucepan over medium heat and bring to a simmer. Add the grits and stir constantly, then add the corn, jalapeños, and cheeses and cook for about 5 minutes. Season the grits with salt and black pepper and set aside until ready to serve.

In a sauté pan, heat 3 tablespoons peanut oil until hot. Cook the cakes for 4 minutes on each side, or until they become golden brown. Remove the cakes from the pan and drain on a paper towel.

To serve, place a quarter of the kale on each plate and top with ¼ cup of grits and a crabcake. Spoon the tomato butter around the cake.

1 pound lump crabmeat
½ yellow onion, diced
1 large egg
3 tablespoons chopped scallions
Juice of 1 lemon
1 cup bread crumbs
1 tablespoon chopped parsley
Salt and black pepper
3 dashes Tabasco sauce
1 bunch kale, stemmed
2 tablespoons unsalted butter
3 tablespoons peanut oil

JALAPEÑO GRITS
2 cups chicken stock
1 cup heavy cream
2 tablespoons unsalted butter
¾ cup instant grits
¼ cup frozen corn, thawed
2 jalapeños, seeded and diced
¼ cup grated Parmesan cheese
¼ cup grated white cheddar cheese
Salt and black pepper

TOMATO BUTTER
(page 161)

Warm Lobster Tacos
with yellow tomato salsa and jicama salad

SERVES 4

YELLOW TOMATO SALSA

2 pints yellow cherry tomatoes, or
    1 pound yellow tomatoes
1 large shallot, finely minced
1 large clove garlic, finely minced
2 tablespoons finely minced cilantro
1 tablespoon Champagne vinegar
2 serrano chiles, seeded and minced
2 teaspoons fresh lime juice
Salt
1 tablespoon maple syrup, if needed

TACOS

Salt
4 (1-pound) lobsters
8 (7-inch) fresh flour tortillas
3 tablespoons corn oil
1 cup grated jalapeño jack cheese
1 cup spinach leaves, washed and
    shredded

JICAMA SALAD

½ small jicama, peeled and cut into
    thin strips
½ small red bell pepper, seeded and
    membranes removed, cut into
    thin strips
½ small yellow bell pepper, seeded
    and membranes removed, cut into
    thin strips
½ small zucchini, cored and seeded,
    cut into thin strips
½ small carrot, peeled and cut into
    thin strips
4 tablespoons peanut oil
2 tablespoons fresh lime juice
Salt
Cayenne pepper

To make the salsa, pulse the tomatoes in a food processor until they are well chopped, but do not puree them. In a mixing bowl, combine the tomatoes and their juices with the shallot, garlic, cilantro, vinegar, chiles, lime juice, and salt to taste and mix well. Add the maple syrup, if needed, to balance the flavors and lightly sweeten the salsa. Cover the salsa and refrigerate for at least 2 hours before serving.

To make the tacos, preheat the oven to 300 degrees F. Fill a large stockpot with lightly salted water and bring to a boil over high heat. Add the lobsters to the boiling water and cook for about 8 minutes. Drain the lobsters and allow them to cool slightly. Wrap the tortillas tightly in foil and warm them in the preheated oven for about 15 minutes. Remove the tortillas from the oven, set aside, and keep warm until ready to use.

Remove the meat from the lobster tails, being careful not to tear the tails apart. Cut the meat into thin medallions (or a medium-size dice, if the meat breaks apart). Heat the corn oil in a sauté pan over medium heat and sauté the lobster medallions until they are just heated through.

To assemble the jicama salad, combine the jicama, bell peppers, zucchini, carrot, oil, and lime juice in a large mixing bowl, and season with salt and cayenne to taste. Toss to mix well.

To serve, spoon equal portions of the warm lobster medallions into the center of each warm tortilla. Sprinkle the lobster with equal portions of grated cheese and shredded spinach. Roll the tortillas into a cylinder shape and place each tortilla on a warm serving plate. Surround the taco with the salsa and garnish each side with a small amount of the salad.

This is a historic Mansion classic. It has been very, very popular and, along with the Tortilla Soup, has remained on the menu for a long time.

Duck Confit Quesadillas *with cilantro pesto*

SERVES 4

BRAISED DUCK LEGS
4 duck legs
Salt and black pepper
1 tablespoon canola oil
1 yellow onion, sliced
2 carrots, chopped
3 cloves garlic, crushed
1 dried ancho chile, stemmed and
   seeded
1 chipotle pepper (canned)
2 teaspoons cumin seeds
1 tablespoon dried Mexican oregano
12 cups chicken stock
½ cup sliced scallions
2 cups grated jalapeño jack cheese

CILANTRO PESTO
2 bunches cilantro, washed and
   stemmed
3 cloves garlic
½ cup pistachios
½ cup grated Parmesan cheese
½ cup olive oil
Salt and black pepper

GUACAMOLE
1 avocado, pitted
1 teaspoon chopped chives
3 dashes Tabasco
2 teaspoons chopped cilantro
Juice of ½ lemon
Salt and black pepper

CUMIN CRÈME FRÂICHE
½ cup crème fraîche
1½ teaspoons ground cumin
1 teaspoon fresh lime juice
Salt

8 (8-inch) flour tortillas
5 tablespoons unsalted butter,
   softened
1 tablespoon chopped chives

Preheat the oven to 350 degrees F. Season each side of the duck legs with salt and black pepper. Heat the oil in a wide, 4-quart braising pot over medium heat and sear each side of the duck legs. Remove the legs and set aside. Add the onion, carrots, and garlic and cook for 6 minutes, or until caramelized. Add the ancho chile, chipotle, cumin, and oregano, stir, and return the duck legs to the pot. Add the chicken stock to cover, bring to a simmer, and cover the pot with parchment paper. Transfer the pot to the preheated oven and braise for 1 hour.

Remove the duck legs from the oven. Using a slotted spoon, carefully remove the duck legs from the pan and allow them to cool to room temperature on a sheet tray.

Strain and reserve the stock, discarding the vegetables. Cook the stock over medium heat for 50 minutes, or until the liquid thickens to a syrup. (You may transfer the liquid to a smaller pot and reduce the heat as the liquid nears the syrup stage.) Transfer the syrup to a ceramic 2-ounce ramekin.

When the duck has cooled, pull the meat and discard the bones and tendons. Place the meat in a medium mixing bowl, add the reduced syrup, and season with salt and black pepper. Add the sliced scallions and cheese and mix well.

To make the cilantro pesto, blend the cilantro, garlic, pistachios, Parmesan cheese, and olive oil in a blender to incorporate. Season with salt and black pepper to taste and set aside.

To make the guacamole, remove the avocado flesh from the peel. Transfer the avocado flesh to a bowl and smash with a fork. Add the chives, Tabasco, cilantro, lemon juice, and salt and pepper to taste. Mix well and set aside.

To make the cumin crème fraîche, whip the crème fraîche, cumin, and lime juice until the mixture thickens to the consistency of sour cream. Season with salt to taste and set aside.

Heat a 10-inch nonstick skillet over medium heat. Lay out the flour tortillas on a cutting board and spread a layer of pesto over four of the eight tortillas. Spread a layer of the duck mixture on top of the pesto. Place the remaining tortillas on top and press down slightly. Brush the top of the tortillas with the softened butter and place one quesadilla, buttered-side down, into the pan. Cook for 3 to 5 minutes, or until golden brown, then flip the quesadilla over using a wide spatula. Cook the other side until golden and return the finished quesadilla to the cutting board. Repeat this with the remaining three quesadillas.

Cut each quesadilla into eight pieces and stack the pieces in the middle of four plates. Garnish with the guacamole, cumin crème fraîche, and chives and serve.

Potted Duck and Foie Gras
with grilled country bread

YIELDS 4 (8-OUNCE) JARS

POTTED DUCK AND FOIE GRAS

1 pound fresh duck foie gras
1 tablespoon salt
2 teaspoons black pepper
¼ cup brandy
1 teaspoon Chinese five spice
1 tablespoon unsalted butter
3¾ tablespoons minced shallot
4 duck legs, boned, skin removed, meat cut into strips
¼ pound chicken livers
¼ pound uncured bacon, diced
¼ cup dry white wine
1 sprig fresh thyme

GRILLED COUNTRY BREAD

1 large round sourdough loaf
Olive oil
Salt

Gherkins or other pickled vegetables

Remove the foie gras from the refrigerator and allow it to soften at room temperature for about 30 minutes. With a spoon, gently open the foie gras and devein it. Place it in a deep dish and season with the salt, pepper, brandy, and Chinese five spice. Cover the foie gras with plastic wrap and allow it to marinate in the refrigerator for 1 hour. After it has chilled, cut the foie gras into large chunks.

Heat the butter in a sauté pan over low heat and cook the shallot for about 5 minutes, or until translucent. Cool and set aside.

In a bowl, combine the duck legs, chicken livers, bacon, white wine, thyme leaves, and cooked shallot. Season the mixture with salt and black pepper to taste, cover with plastic wrap, and allow to rest in the refrigerator for 1 hour. Remove from the refrigerator, pass the mixture through a meat grinder, and reserve.

Fill four 8-ounce hinged glass jars with large chunks of the foie gras and the meat mixture, alternating the two mixtures to create layers in the jar. Close and seal the jars and place them in a large stockpot. Cover the jars with water and place dish towels in the pot to prevent the jars from knocking together. Bring the water to a boil slowly and continue to boil for 45 minutes. Carefully remove the jars from the water and allow them to cool completely. The jars can be stored in the refrigerator for months.

To make the grilled country bread, cut the sourdough loaf into ½-inch-thick slices. Drizzle with a little olive oil on both sides and sprinkle with a pinch of salt. Heat the slices on a hot grill just long enough to create grill marks on each side.

Serve the potted duck and foie gras with grilled country bread, gherkins, or pickled vegetables.

Soups & Salads

Tortilla Soup

Chilled Cantaloupe Soup

Black Bean and Jalapeño Jack Soups

Artichoke Soup

Silky Corn Soup

Sunchoke Soup

Spiced Carrot Soup

King Crab Soup and Sweet Potato Tortellini

Heirloom Tomato Composition

Red Jalapeño Caesar Salad

Watermelon Salad

Crab Cobb Salad

Lobster Salad

Warm Potato Salad

Crispy Fried Oysters and Spinach Salad

Paula Lambert's Roasted Beet and Goat Cheese Salad

Mansion Salad

Tortilla Soup

SERVES 6

6 Roma tomatoes
½ medium onion, peeled and
thinly sliced
1 New Mexico chile, seeded
8 cups low-sodium chicken stock
3 tablespoons plus about ½ cup
canola oil
2 cloves garlic, peeled and crushed
1 tablespoon cumin seeds
1 sprig fresh thyme
½ tablespoon dried oregano
½ teaspoon coriander seeds
1 large bay leaf
1 tablespoon tomato paste
1 jalapeño pepper, chopped
(seeded for milder soup)
6 small corn tortillas, quartered
2 epazote leaves, or fresh Mexican
oregano (see note)
Salt
Juice of 1 lemon
Cayenne pepper

GARNISH
1 boneless, skinless chicken breast
4 cups chicken stock
4 cups vegetable oil
2 corn tortillas, cut into
2 x ½-inch strips
Salt
1 ripe avocado, cut into ½-inch cubes
2 ounces aged cheddar cheese,
shredded

Combine the tomatoes and onion in a blender and puree. Pour the puree into a bowl and set aside.

Roast the New Mexico chile in a 375-degree-F oven for 3 to 4 minutes. In a blender, puree the chile with 1 cup chicken stock. Pour the mixture into a bowl and set aside.

Heat 1 tablespoon of canola oil in a medium sauté pan over high heat and toast the garlic, cumin seeds, thyme, dried oregano, and coriander seeds, stirring, until golden and fragrant. Set the toasted spice mixture aside in a small bowl.

Heat 2 tablespoons of canola oil in a large stockpot over high heat. Add the onion and tomato puree and cook for 5 minutes. Add the remaining chicken stock, the bay leaf, tomato paste, chile puree, jalapeño, and the toasted spice mixture.

In a Dutch oven or heavy skillet, add just enough oil to cover the quartered tortillas (do not add the tortillas to the pot at this point), and heat the oil to 350 degrees F. When the oil is hot, fry the quartered tortillas for 2 to 4 minutes, or until crisp. Drain the fried quarters on paper towels, add them to the stockpot, and bring the mixture to a boil. Lower the heat and simmer for 1 hour, skimming off the fat as necessary. In the last 10 minutes of cooking, add the epazote leaves or fresh oregano. Process the soup in a food mill, or use a blender to obtain a smooth consistency, and return the soup to the stockpot to keep warm. If the soup becomes too thick, add additional chicken stock to thin it out. Season the soup with salt, lemon juice, and cayenne to taste.

Just before serving, prepare the garnish. In a separate stockpot, poach the chicken breast in the chicken stock over low heat for 15 minutes, then cut into ½-inch cubes. In a Dutch oven or heavy skillet, heat 4 cups vegetable oil to 350 degrees F. Fry the tortilla strips for 2 minutes, or until golden brown. Drain the strips on paper towels and season with salt.

To serve, warm the chicken and avocado cubes up slowly in a little bit of the tortilla soup, then divide evenly among four soup bowls. Pour the hot tortilla soup over each bowl and top with the cheddar cheese and fried tortilla strips, or serve on the side.

Note: Epazote is a pungent Mexican herb available in Mexican specialty stores. If epazote isn't available, you can substitute fresh Mexican oregano.

  This is the Mansion's signature dish. Bill Cosby had it delivered to the airport when he didn't have time to dine with us before a flight. Marvin Hamlish orders a bowl every time he checks in.

Chilled Cantaloupe Soup
with grapefruit and watermelon

2 ripe cantaloupes, peeled, seeded,
   and chopped
4 ounces fresh raspberries
Juice of 1 lemon
1 ounce dry vermouth
½ ripe seedless watermelon, peeled
   and cut in ⅓-inch cubes
½ ripe honeydew melon, peeled,
   seeded, and cut in ⅓-inch cubes
1 ruby red grapefruit, segmented
1 teaspoon sea salt
2 ½ tablespoons sugar
8 fresh mint leaves, minced
Zest of 1 lime
2 tablespoons extra virgin olive oil

Combine the cantaloupe, half the raspberries, the lemon juice, and vermouth in a blender and process until smooth. Pour the mixture into a bowl, cover, and refrigerate for at least 1 hour.

Combine the watermelon, honeydew, grapefruit, salt, sugar, and mint in a large mixing bowl. Cover and macerate in the refrigerator for 30 minutes.

To serve, scoop the watermelon-honeydew mixture into the center of each very cold soup bowl and pour the chilled cantaloupe mixture around the melons. Top the soup with a pinch of lime zest, a drizzle of olive oil, and a few whole fresh raspberries. Serve immediately; the soup is best served very cold.

Black Bean and Jalapeño Jack Soups
with roasted pepper creams

BLACK BEAN SOUP

1 cup dried black beans
1 onion, chopped
3 cloves garlic, chopped
1 jalapeño, seeded and chopped
1 small leek (white part only), chopped
1 stalk celery, chopped
4 sprigs fresh cilantro
4 cups chicken stock or broth
1 cup ham scraps or 1 large ham bone
Salt
Black pepper
Juice of 1 lemon

JALAPEÑO JACK SOUP

2 tablespoons vegetable oil
1 onion, chopped
1 small leek (white part only), chopped
1 stalk celery, chopped
2 cloves garlic, chopped
1½ cups flat beer
1 cup white wine
Sachet (1 bay leaf, 5 sprigs fresh thyme, 1 tablespoon white peppercorns)
4 cups chicken stock
1 jalapeño, seeded and chopped
2 tablespoons unsalted butter, softened
2 tablespoons flour
1 cup shredded jalapeño jack cheese

¼ cup heavy cream
Salt
Black pepper
Juice of 1 lemon

ROASTED RED AND YELLOW PEPPER CREAMS

1 roasted red bell pepper, stemmed and seeded
1 roasted yellow bell pepper, stemmed and seeded
¼ cup very cold heavy cream
½ cup sour cream
Salt
Fresh lime juice

To make the black bean soup, rinse the beans and discard any that are shriveled. In a large bowl, soak the beans for 2 to 3 hours in enough cold water to cover. Drain the beans. Place the soaked beans, onion, garlic, jalapeño, leek, celery, cilantro, chicken stock, and ham in a large stockpot and bring to a boil over high heat. Lower the heat and simmer for about 2 hours or until the beans are very soft, frequently skimming foam off the top.

When the beans are soft, remove the ham scraps or bone. Pour the beans into a blender or food processor (in batches if necessary) and blend until smooth. Strain the mixture, return the soup to the stockpot, and season to taste with salt, pepper, and lemon juice. The soup should be thick, but if it is too thick for your taste, use additional hot chicken stock to thin it out. Keep warm until ready to serve.

To make the jalapeño jack soup, heat the oil in a large sauté pan over medium heat. Sauté the onion, leek, celery, and garlic for 5 minutes, or until soft. Add the beer and wine and bring to a boil. Cook for 10 minutes, or until the liquid is reduced by half. Make a sachet by bundling together the bay leaf, thyme, and peppercorns in a cheesecloth and securing it with butcher string. Add the chicken stock, jalapeño, and sachet to the pan and bring to a boil. Skim the foam from the top, reduce the heat, and simmer for about 1 hour. Remove the sachet.

 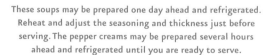

These soups may be prepared one day ahead and refrigerated. Reheat and adjust the seasoning and thickness just before serving. The pepper creams may be prepared several hours ahead and refrigerated until you are ready to serve.

Knead together the butter and flour. Slowly whisk the mixture into the soup and blend until smooth. Simmer for an additional 30 minutes. Remove the pan from the heat and immediately stir in the cheese and heavy cream, and whisk until smooth.

Place the liquid in a blender or food processor (in batches if necessary) and blend until smooth. Strain the mixture, return it to the pan, and season to taste with salt, pepper, and lemon juice. The soup should be very thick, but if it is too thick, thin it out with additional hot chicken stock.

Roast the peppers on a preheated fire grill for 5 minutes on each side to char the skin. Place the peppers in a mixing bowl and cover with plastic wrap. Set aside for 1 hour. When cool enough to handle, peel the skin off the peppers and seed and stem them.

To make the red pepper cream, puree the roasted red pepper in a food processor or blender, using the steel blade, until smooth. Add 2 tablespoons cream and ¼ cup sour cream. Process the mixture briefly to combine. Season to taste with salt and lime juice. Strain the cream through a fine sieve, pour into a squeeze bottle, and set aside. Clean the bowl of the food processor and repeat the process using the roasted yellow pepper and the remaining cream and sour cream. Pour the cream into another squeeze bottle and set aside.

To serve, slowly pour both hot soups into a bowl side by side to achieve a clear line of division between the two soups. Squeeze the roasted pepper creams on top in a pretty design and serve.

Artichoke Soup
with Parmesan truffle fritters

To make the fritter batter, combine the cheese, sour cream, truffle, truffle oil, and egg yolks in a mixing bowl and stir to a smooth paste consistency. Cover the batter with plastic wrap and refrigerate for 30 minutes.

Place the artichokes in a large stockpot and cover with water. Boil, covered, over medium heat for 30 minutes. Remove the artichokes from the water and allow them to cool. When cool, remove the tough outer leaves and reserve only the soft, edible artichoke hearts. Cut the hearts into 1-inch cubes and set aside.

In a large saucepot over medium heat, cook the onion and garlic in the olive oil for 5 minutes, or until the onion is translucent and soft. Be careful not to brown or caramelize the onion. Add the artichokes and white wine and cook until all the liquid has evaporated. Add the vegetable stock and cook for 20 minutes. Puree the soup in a blender and pass it through a sieve. Return the soup to the saucepot and season with a pinch of salt and black pepper to taste. Keep the soup warm until you are ready to serve.

Just before serving, fry the fritters. Heat the canola oil to 375 degrees F. Use a small scoop to form balls of the chilled batter and roll each ball in the bread crumbs. Fry the fritters in batches until they turn golden brown and drain them on a paper towel.

Serve each bowl of hot artichoke soup with a few fritters and garnish with sour cream and a drizzle of olive oil.

PARMESAN TRUFFLE FRITTERS
4 ounces Parmesan cheese, grated
½ cup sour cream
1 tablespoon chopped black truffle
  peelings
½ teaspoon truffle oil
4 egg yolks
Canola oil
¼ cup panko (Japanese bread crumbs)

ARTICHOKE SOUP
4 artichokes
1 cup sliced white onion
1 clove garlic, chopped
2 tablespoons extra virgin olive oil,
  plus more for garnish
⅓ cup white wine
6 cups vegetable stock
Salt and black pepper
Sour cream, for garnish

The cast of the hit television show *Dallas* loved to stay at the Mansion, and Victoria Principal chose to have her wedding here.

Silky Corn Soup *with morel mushrooms*

SERVES 4

2 tablespoons minced shallot
2 tablespoons unsalted butter
1 pound fresh morel mushrooms,
    washed and stemmed
⅓ cup dry white wine
1 cup chicken stock (may substitute
    vegetable stock for a vegetarian
    soup)
Salt
Black pepper
4 ears fresh corn on the cob, kernels
    cut off, cobs reserved
½ cup sliced white onion
1 clove garlic, crushed
2 tablespoons olive oil
1 tablespoon honey
2 tablespoons sour cream
1 tablespoon minced fresh chives
Croutons, optional

In a sauté pan over medium heat, sweat the shallot in the butter for 2 minutes. Add the cleaned morels and cook for 1 minute. Add the white wine and cook until all of the liquid has evaporated. When dry, add the chicken stock and cook for 6 minutes, or until the mushrooms are tender. Season with a pinch of salt and black pepper and set aside until ready to serve.

In a stockpot, boil the corn cobs slowly in 8 cups of water for 25 minutes. When done, discard the cobs and reserve the cooking liquid.

In a separate saucepot over medium heat, sauté the onion and garlic in the olive oil for 5 minutes. Add the honey and the corn kernels and cook for 5 more minutes. Add the cooking liquid from the corn cobs and cook for 25 minutes more. Puree the hot soup in a blender until it is smooth and silky, then pass it through a sieve. Return the soup to the saucepot and season with a pinch of salt and black pepper.

To serve, pour the hot soup into four bowls and top with the warm morels. Garnish each bowl with ½ tablespoon of sour cream and a pinch of chives. If desired, serve with croutons for a crunchy texture.

This is a very hearty soup. You can replace the morel mushrooms with shiitakes if desired. If you use morels, wash them three times in cold water to remove all of the sand.

Sunchoke Soup *with glazed boneless chicken wings*

SERVES 4

In a stockpot, combine 4 cups chicken stock, the thyme, bay leaf, garlic, and a pinch of salt and black pepper. Bring to a boil and cook for 5 minutes. Add the chicken wings, reduce the heat to low, and cook for another 20 minutes. Remove the wings from the cooking liquid and allow them to cool, reserving the cooking liquid. Once the wings are cool, remove the bones.

In a saucepot over medium heat, cook the shallots and leek in the olive oil for 3 minutes, or until they are translucent. Add the sunchokes and cook for 5 minutes. Add the remaining chicken stock and cooking liquid from the wings and cook for another 30 minutes. Puree the soup in a blender and pass it through a sieve. Return the soup to the saucepot and season with salt and black pepper. Keep the soup warm until you are ready to serve.

In a sauté pan over medium heat, brown the chicken wings on each side in the butter. When brown, add the lemon juice, toss the chicken to coat, and season it with salt and black pepper.

To serve, top the hot soup with 3 glazed chicken wings in each bowl and garnish with whipped cream.

8 cups chicken stock
1 teaspoon fresh thyme
1 bay leaf
1 clove garlic, crushed
Salt
Black pepper
12 chicken wings, midsection only
½ cup sliced shallots
1 leek, washed and minced
2 tablespoons olive oil
2 pounds sunchokes, peeled and sliced
4 tablespoons (½ stick) unsalted
   butter
Juice of 1 lemon
2 tablespoons heavy cream,
   whipped, for garnish

Spiced Carrot Soup *with Gulf shrimp ravioli*

SERVES 4

RAVIOLI DOUGH
2 cups all-purpose flour, plus more
    for dusting
½ cup semolina flour
3 eggs
1 egg yolk
2 tablespoons extra virgin olive oil
1 teaspoon salt

RAVIOLI FILLING
1 pound shrimp, peeled, deveined,
    and chopped
1 tablespoon chopped cilantro
½ tablespoon chopped ginger
1 clove garlic, chopped
1 teaspoon sesame oil
Zest of 1 lemon
Salt
Black pepper

SOUP
¾ cup sliced white onion
2 tablespoons olive oil, plus more
    for garnish
1 pound carrots, peeled and
    roughly chopped
1 teaspoon ground cumin
1 tablespoon honey
8 cups vegetable stock
1 star anise
½ cinnamon stick
1 dried arbol chile
Salt and black pepper

To make the pasta dough, combine the flours, eggs, egg yolk, olive oil, and 1 teaspoon salt in a standing mixer and mix to form a gummy ball. Be careful to not overmix. Using a pasta machine, roll the dough into two very thin sheets, dusting with flour as necessary to avoid sticking.

To make the filling, combine the shrimp, cilantro, ginger, garlic, sesame oil, lemon zest, and a pinch of salt and black pepper in a mixing bowl. Spoon an equal amount of the shrimp mixture in four rows of four mounds of shrimp filling, evenly spaced on one sheet of pasta. Top with the second sheet of pasta. Cut the ravioli out using a cookie cutter or cut into squares using a paring knife. Seal the edges of each ravioli around the mounds of shrimp filling by pinching the dough together.

In a large stockpot, cook the onions in the olive oil for 5 minutes, or until they become soft and translucent. Add the carrots, cumin, and honey and cook for 5 minutes. Add the vegetable stock, star anise, cinnamon stick, and chile and cook for 25 minutes, or until the carrots are soft. Remove the star anise and cinnamon stick. Puree the soup in a blender to achieve a silky consistency, then pass it through a sieve. Return the soup to the stockpot and season with a pinch of salt and pepper. Keep the soup warm until you are ready to serve.

Bring a second large stockpot of water to a boil and season it with generously with salt. Add the ravioli and cook for 3 minutes. Drain the ravioli in a colander.

Serve the hot carrot soup with 4 ravioli in each bowl and garnish with a drizzle of olive oil.

King Crab Soup and Sweet Potato *Tortellini* with lemon Thai basil

SERVES 4

CRAB SOUP BASE

2½ pounds live blue crabs, washed
    and halved
¼ cup unsalted butter
1 carrot, chopped
2 large shallots, sliced
1 head garlic, halved
2 ribs celery, chopped
1 cup chardonnay
6 cups chicken stock or broth
½ bulb fennel, green parts only,
    cleaned and chopped
1 dried arbol chile
Salt and black pepper

BUTTERNUT SQUASH SOUP

1 butternut squash
Salt
Black pepper
½ teaspoon Chinese five spice
½ cup (1 stick) unsalted butter
½ yellow onion, thinly sliced
½ bulb fennel, thinly sliced
1 tablespoon canola oil
2 cups chicken stock

HERB SACHET

1 teaspoon fennel seeds
1 teaspoon coriander seeds
2 star anise
½ teaspoon Szechuan peppercorns
1 teaspoon black peppercorns
2 cloves garlic
3 whole cloves
1 sprig thyme

TORTELLINI

1 sweet potato
2 tablespoons canola oil
1 teaspoon Chinese five spice
1 tablespoon unsalted butter
1 tablespoon extra virgin olive oil
Salt and black pepper
1 to 2 prepared fresh pasta sheets
1 egg, lightly beaten

CRAB SOUP

2 tablespoons unslated butter
½ pound king crab leg meat,
    cut into 1-inch pieces
1 tablespoon pantai crab paste
    (found in Asian markets)
¼ cup chicken stock
Salt and black pepper
Petite lemon Thai basil, for garnish

To make the crab soup base, cook the crabs in a large stockpot over medium heat until they turn red. Add the butter and cook for 20 to 30 minutes, or until the bodies are lightly caramelized. Add the carrots, shallots, garlic, and celery and cook for 20 minutes, or until the vegetables are tender. Add the white wine and simmer for 30 to 40 minutes, or until the liquid is reduced by half. Cover with the chicken stock, add the fennel and chiles, and cook for 1½ hours more. When done, mash the crab bodies with a wooden spoon, pass the soup through a fine-mesh strainer into a medium-sized bowl, and discard the solids. Season with salt and black pepper and set aside.

To make the butternut squash soup, preheat the oven to 350 degrees F. Cut the squash in half lengthwise and use a spoon to remove the seeds. Score the flesh with a knife and season with salt, black pepper, and Chinese five spice. Place on a baking sheet, flesh side up, and top with large pats of butter. Cover the pan with foil and roast in the oven until tender, 1 to 1½ hours. Remove the squash from the oven, allow it to cool, then scoop out the flesh and set it aside.

In a large stockpot over medium heat, cook the onion and fennel in the canola oil for 10 to 12 minutes, or until the onion is soft and translucent. Make a sachet by bundling all of the ingredients in a cheesecloth and tying it with butcher string. Add 2 cups chicken stock and the herb sachet to the stockpot and cook for 30 to 40 minutes. Add the squash flesh and cook for 10 more minutes. Remove and discard the sachet. Puree the hot soup in a blender until smooth and set aside in a bowl.

Keep the oven temperature at 350 degrees F. Rub the sweet potato lightly with the canola oil and bake for 45 minutes to 1 hour, or until tender. Allow the potato to cool and remove the peel. Combine the sweet potato flesh, Chinese five spice, 1 tablespoon butter, and olive oil in the bowl of a food processor and process until smooth. Add salt and black pepper to taste, and transfer the mixture to a pastry bag.

Using a 2-inch round cutter, cut twelve circles of pasta and brush with the beaten egg. Pipe about 1 tablespoon of filling onto one side of each of the circles, leaving room at the edge. Fold the pasta over to cover the potato puree and seal the edges

to create a half-moon shape. Brush each tortellini again with the beaten egg. Place your forefinger under the straight edge of the semicircle. Gently raise your finger up, pull the two corners of the pasta together around your finger, and pinch the edges together to seal. As you do this, the circular edge of the half-moon will turn up to form the tortellini, which resembles the brim of a hat turned up.

Boil 4 cups of generously salted water in a 2-quart saucepan. Drop the tortellini in the boiling water and cook for 3 to 5 minutes. The tortellini are done when they begin to float.

In a sauté pan over medium heat, combine 2 tablespoons butter, the crab meat, crab paste, and ¼ cup chicken stock and cook for 4 minutes. Season with salt and pepper to taste. Add the cooked tortellini and toss together to combine. In a separate saucepan over medium heat, add 4 cups crab soup base and 4 cups butternut squash soup and heat to a boil.

To serve, divide the crab meat among four bowls and top with 3 tortellini each. Garnish with lemon Thai basil. Pour the hot soup over the tortellini from a pitcher at tableside, for a special presentation.

Tom Spicer / THE SPICE OF LIFE

VEGETABLES ARE TOM SPICER'S DESTINY. He grew up in New Orleans, the youngest in a family of seven children, and spent his early years ferreting out nooks and crannies in the five acres of lush fields and woods that surrounded his parents' three-story house just outside the city. Live oak, towering magnolias, 200-year-old pecans, and mulberry trees cast their shadows; ferns, climbing roses, and tangles of honeysuckle vines flourished in fragrant, lacy layers; and blackberry brambles, and banana, pomegranate, and fig trees offered their fruit. "I could explore and still feel safe," he says. The profusion cast its spell: "It gave me a taste for the exotic." Not that the taste wasn't already lurking in the Spicer genes. Tom's sister, Susan Spicer, is now an award-winning chef at Bayona and Herbsaint restaurants in New Orleans. Spicer's great-grandfather was the personal gardener for the Vanderbilt family and cultivated strawberries and melons in their greenhouses in Rhode Island for enjoyment during winters. "I think that an interest in gardening is in my blood," opines Spicer.

The Spice Man, as he is known to everybody, moved to Dallas in the mid-eighties on the advice of a culinary friend: "He said, 'You have to come here. This is where it's all happening.' " Now Spicer operates his own garden in Dallas from which he supplies the Mansion with herbs for salads and seasonings for many dishes. "You can almost walk out the Mansion's back door and touch my place with a fork," says Spicer about the plot. It flourishes in Technicolor splendor behind Spicer's store where local chefs and home cooks come to shop for wholesale produce just pulled out of the ground. "Sometimes the line stretches around the block," he says. "This is the epitome of garden to table." The farmer is justifiably proud of the 11,000 square feet he has beguiled into producing about fifteen times as much as other plots the same size. Braising greens, baby carrots in mixed colors, watermelon radishes, French breakfast radishes, baby fennel, baby pearled leeks, mache, and other lettuces are in their element. "If you know how to grow intensively," Spicer explains, "you can do it. But it's taken me 27 years to perfect my technique." Is it just technique that explains Spicer's gift for raising vegetables? The urban farmer has a better theory: "I think," he says, "it's genetic."

Heirloom Tomato Composition
with Tom Spicer's fresh herbs

SERVES 4

To make the Romesco condiment, preheat the oven to 350 degrees F. Toss the tomatoes with 2 tablespoons extra virgin olive oil and a pinch of salt and pepper and lay on a cookie sheet, skin side up. Roast for 25 minutes, or until the tomatoes have caramelized. Remove the skin and set the tomato flesh aside.

Increase the oven temperature to 375 degrees F. Spread the pine nuts and almonds on a cookie sheet and toast in the oven for 15 minutes, or until golden brown. Set aside.

Heat 1 tablespoon extra virgin olive oil in a medium sauté pan over medium heat and cook the shallots and garlic until they become soft and translucent—do not allow them to brown. Add the roasted tomatoes, chile flakes, and paprika and stir. Add the sherry vinegar, reduce the heat to low, and stir well, scraping the bottom of the pan. Cook slowly until the mixture is reduced to a paste.

In a blender, combine the tomato mixture, nuts, and 1 tablespoon olive oil and process until smooth. Season with a pinch of salt and pepper and set aside.

To make the dressing, combine the tomatoes, tomato paste, sherry vinegar, olive oil, salt, and pepper in a blender and puree until smooth.

To assemble the salad, arrange the tomatoes on four salad plates. Garnish each plate with 1 tablespoon of Romesco condiment, and drizzle the tomatoes with 1 tablespoon of tomato dressing and extra virgin olive oil. Season with salt and cracked black pepper and drizzle with balsamic vinegar. Garnish with the mixed herbs and serve.

ROMESCO CONDIMENT

4 Roma tomatoes, halved
4 tablespoons extra virgin olive oil
Salt and black pepper
1 tablespoon pine nuts
1 tablespoon whole almonds
2 shallots, chopped
1 clove garlic, chopped
½ teaspoon chile flakes
1 teaspoon smoked paprika
2 tablespoons sherry vinegar

TOMATO DRESSING

2 Roma tomatoes, cubed
1 teaspoon tomato paste
1 tablespoon sherry vinegar
3 tablespoons extra virgin olive oil
Pinch salt
Pinch pepper

SALAD

2 pounds heirloom tomatoes, cut
   into ½-inch slices
3 tablespoons extra virgin olive oil
½ tablespoon sea salt
½ tablespoon cracked black
   peppercorns
2 tablespoons aged balsamic vinegar
½ cup fresh herb mix (basil, chives,
   and parsley), for garnish

 There are hundreds of varieties of heirloom tomatoes in varying flavors and colors. At the Mansion, we like to use Brandywine, green zebra, and purple flesh tomatoes because of their pretty color and flavor variety.

Red Jalapeño Caesar Salad
with diablo Gulf shrimp

SERVES 4

DIABLO SAUCE
¼ cup sushi vinegar
½ (7-ounce) can roasted red peppers, drained
½ habanero pepper, split, seeded, and stemmed
¼ large yellow onion, sliced
1 inch ginger root, peeled and chopped
2 cloves garlic, chopped
½ shallot, chopped
2 tablespoons orange juice
¼ mango, peeled, pitted, and pureed
½ teaspoon maple syrup
Fresh lime juice

RED JALAPEÑO CAESAR DRESSING
2 large egg yolks
4 cloves smoked garlic, minced
2 shallots, minced
4 anchovy fillets
2 tablespoons hot mustard
1 tablespoon Worcestershire sauce
2 teaspoons Tabasco sauce
2 teaspoons balsamic vinegar
¾ cup canola oil
¾ cup olive oil
4 roasted red jalapeños, chopped
1 tablespoon chopped cilantro
2 tablespoons fresh lime juice
Salt and cracked black pepper

SALAD
4 heads romaine lettuce, washed and roughly chopped
¼ cup cotija cheese (found in Mexican specialty stores)
12 (16/20) Gulf shrimp, peeled and deveined
¼ cup chopped pepitas (squash or pumpkin seeds)

To make the diablo sauce, combine the vinegar, roasted red peppers, habanero, onion, ginger, garlic, shallots, orange juice, mango, maple syrup, and lime juice to taste in a heavy saucepan. Cook over low to medium heat for 1 hour. Transfer to a blender and puree for 5 minutes. Strain the puree through a conical strainer and set aside.

To make the dressing, combine the egg yolks, garlic, shallots, anchovies, mustard, Worcestershire sauce, Tabasco sauce, and balsamic vinegar in a blender. Puree until smooth. Slowly add the oils until the dressing is emulsified and creamy. Add the chopped jalapeños, cilantro, lime juice, and salt and black pepper to taste. Set aside. The dressing can be kept in the refrigerator for two weeks.

To assemble the salad, combine the lettuce, 1 cup of red jalapeño Caesar dressing, and the cheese in a large mixing bowl and massage the dressing into the lettuce with both hands until well coated. In four large round plates or very shallow chilled bowls, divide the salad into equal portions.

In a large sauté pan over medium heat, add ½ cup diablo sauce and the shrimp and sauté for 5 minutes, or until the shrimp are cooked through. Pull the shrimp out with a slotted spoon and drain on a paper towel. Put 3 shrimp on the side of each dish. Sprinkle the remaining cotija cheese on each salad, garnish with a sprinkle of the chopped pepitas, and serve.

Watermelon Salad with feta cheese, pink peppercorn—cilantro vinaigrette, and crispy prosciutto

SERVES 4

To make the candied lemon zest, zest both lemons using a zester, creating long thin strips of yellow skin only (no white pith). In a small saucepot, boil the lemon zest for 2 minutes.

Drain the liquid and repeat the operation twice to remove any bitterness. Drain the liquid for the final time and combine the blanched lemon zest, sugar, and 4 tablespoons water in the saucepot and cook slowly over low heat for 20 minutes, or until the lemon has reached the consistency of marmalade.

To make the vinaigrette, whisk the pink and black peppercorns, lemon juice, lime zest, cayenne pepper, candied lemon, and olive oil together and set aside.

To dry the prosciutto slices, preheat the oven to 300 degrees F. Line a baking sheet with parchment paper. Lay out the prosciutto slices on the baking sheet and dry them in the oven for 10 to 15 minutes, or until crispy.

To assemble the salad, place the watermelon cubes on a rectangular plate. Season each cube with 1 tablespoon of pink peppercorn vinaigrette and the chopped cilantro. Top with the feta cheese and pickled onion. Crack the dry prosciutto into pieces and garnish the salad. Finish with a few drops of balsamic vinegar and olive oil, the petite arugula, and fleur de sel before serving.

Note: You can make your own pickled onion at least 24 hours in advance. Boil 1 onion in 2 cups water, 1 cup Champagne vinegar, salt, and cracked black peppercorns and then let it cool completely. Cover and refrigerate. Pickled onion will keep, refrigerated, for up to 6 weeks.

CANDIED LEMON ZEST
2 lemons
2 tablespoons sugar

PINK PEPPERCORN VINAIGRETTE
2 tablespoons pink peppercorns
¼ tablespoon black peppercorns
Juice of 1 lemon
Zest of l lime
Pinch cayenne pepper
½ tablespoon candied lemon zest
¼ cup extra virgin olive oil

4 thin slices prosciutto

SALAD
½ small watermelon, cut into
  1-inch cubes
1 tablespoon chopped cilantro
2 ounces feta cheese
Pickled onion (see note)
2 tablespoons aged balsamic vinegar
2 tablespoons extra virgin olive oil
1 handful petite arugula
Fleur de sel

Chef Bruno demonstrated this dish at the State Fair of Texas in 2010.
The secret is in the pink peppercorn dressing. People are always surprised
by the flavor—it's very floral.

MAKING CHEESE IS AN ANCIENT REMEDY—a pre-refrigeration, pre-packaging scheme to persuade milk into lasting a little longer. That first little hunk of cheese was probably a happy accident triggered when nomads domesticated goats and sheep 10,000 years ago. "Packing up" for a nomad meant storing milk in containers fashioned from inflated animal organs and hitting the road, goats in tow. The practice had its merits, and an unanticipated element of magic: natural enzymes (rennet, specifically) obligingly flourish in mammalian stomachs for the sole purpose of digesting mother's milk. The peripatetic hunters and gatherers noticed that the milk they were toting around in cow stomachs would develop delicious lumps and alluring liquids, the aboriginal version of curds and whey.

Fast forward 10,000 years, and not much has changed about the cheesemaking process. Gone is the animal organ storage vessel (replaced by steel vats); and we deliberately add rennet to energize milk into pert little curds. But accident still plays a part, as it did for Rebeccah Durkin, a 31-year-old champion cheesemaker whose feta and blue cheeses are mainstays in the Mansion's kitchen. Chefs at the Mansion are particularly fond of the light and tart feta, a perfect accompaniment to watermelon and used in one of the restaurant's most loved salads.

Durkin grew up in the Homestead Heritage community—an agrarian community of 1,000 people—in the Brazos Valley near Waco. The community's holistic approach to back-to-basics living encourages traditional trades such as pottery and furniture-making, spinning, and raising livestock. "One spring," Durkin says, "we were producing so much milk that it was going to waste." She was 19 at the time, and enterprising. Durkin dug through her bookshelves in search of a book on cheesemaking, a gift from her sister years before. "I started experimenting." Low-tech apparatus at the ready—a stainless-steel bowl and slotted spoon for scooping up curds, Durkin made mozzarella. Buoyed by a favorable response from visitors at Homestead Heritage's Thanksgiving Festival, the budding cheesemaker progressed to feta. Marinated in olive oil, Brazos Valley Marinated Feta Cheese is a best-seller. Packed in a clear glass jar, with dried tomatoes, basil, and garlic, it's a briny brew that's good drizzled over a feta-topped pizza.

By the time Durkin was 26, she'd become a virtuoso. And she'd gone beyond just being a cheesemaker. "My dream was to start a business," she says. At that very moment, in December 2005, Durkin's cousin Marc Kuehl arrived at Homestead Heritage. It was Kuehl who started selling Brazos Valley cheeses to the world at large. Wheels of Gouda, sweet and tart blueberry Havarti, creamy mold-ripened Brazos Select, cheddar, pepper jack, Brie, Parmesan, and more emerged from their ever-expanding facility.

Their secret? "Our cheeses are made from raw milk," says Kuehl. Richly flavored and redolent of grasses, flowers, and herbs the cow lunched on just before it was milked, raw milk is all character. "We don't wax or vacuum package our cheeses," notes Durkin. Instead they are bandage-wrapped in cheesecloth so that the cheeses continue to breathe as they age. At the Mansion, the chef has a fondness for Brazos Valley Munster, which Durkin rubs with a saltwater/*Brevibacterium Linens* solution to encourage the growth of an orange bloomy rind. The result is a full meaty flavor that hints of chocolate. The chef has also developed menu offerings to feature Brazos Valley cheeses: The feta and Texas watermelon salad is a tasty textural tango of sweet and tangy. But for pure luxury, the crab Cobb salad and Brazos Valley blue cheese fritters is a showstopper. And if it's spring, and the cows have wandered through a patch of violets, so much the better.

Crab Cobb Salad *and Brazos Valley*
blue cheese fritters

SERVES 4

BLUE CHEESE FRITTERS
4 ounces Brazos Valley blue cheese
3 tablespoons unsalted butter, softened
½ teaspoon Worcestershire sauce
Salt and black pepper
1 cup flour
4 eggs, beaten
2 cups panko (Japanese bread crumbs)
2 cups grapeseed oil

SALAD
4 large heirloom tomatoes, stemmed and quartered
3 tablespoons extra virgin olive oil
2 tablespoons sherry vinegar
2 shallots, thinly sliced
2 tablespoons chives, cut into ½-inch pieces
Salt and black pepper
4 ripe avocados
Juice of ½ lemon
1 pound jumbo lump crab meat
¼ teaspoon Sriracha hot chile sauce
8 romaine lettuce hearts, halved lengthwise
4 hard-boiled eggs, grated, for garnish

BACON AND SHALLOT VINAIGRETTE
½ pound bacon, chopped
2 shallots, diced small
1 tablespoon Dijon mustard
1 tablespoon whole grain mustard
1 cup canola oil
2 tablespoons sherry vinegar
Salt and black pepper

To make the fritter batter, combine the blue cheese, butter, and Worcestershire sauce in a food processor and process until smooth. Season with salt and black pepper to taste and transfer the mixture to a pastry bag. Pipe the mixture onto a parchment-lined baking sheet to form 1-inch balls. Cover the baking sheet and freeze for 3 hours.

In a medium bowl, season the flour with a pinch of salt and black pepper. In a separate bowl, add the beaten eggs, and use a third bowl for the bread crumbs. Toss the frozen balls in the flour, then dip them in the beaten egg, followed by the bread crumbs to coat completely. Place the balls in a container, cover, and return them to the freezer. These can be prepared ahead and will keep in the freezer in a covered container for one month.

To begin the salad, combine the tomatoes, olive oil, vinegar, shallots, chives, salt, and black pepper in a shallow baking dish. Cover and marinate in the refrigerator for at least 1 hour.

To make the dressing, cook the bacon in a medium saucepan over medium heat until crisp. Remove the bacon, drain on a paper towel, and pat to remove excess grease. Reserve 2 tablespoons bacon grease and sauté the shallots over medium heat until soft.

Pulse the bacon in a food processor 3 to 4 times until it is chopped. Combine the bacon, shallots, mustards, oil, and vinegar in a mixing bowl and whisk well. Season with salt and pepper to taste and set aside.

Remove the pits from the avocados and scoop the flesh into a small bowl. Add the lemon juice and use a fork to smash the avocados to a chunky consistency. Season with a pinch of salt and black pepper.

In another small mixing bowl, combine the crab meat, 2 tablespoons vinaigrette, the Sriracha, salt, and black pepper and mix well.

In a large mixing bowl, toss the romaine hearts with ¼ cup vinaigrette. Season with a pinch of salt and black pepper.

Just before serving, heat the grapeseed oil to 360 degrees F and fry the frozen blue cheese balls, six at a time, for 4 to 6 minutes, or until golden brown. Drain on a paper towel.

To assemble the salad, spread a quarter of the avocado mixture onto the bottom of four chilled salad bowls. Place four marinated tomato wedges around the avocado mixture. Place the romaine hearts in the center of each bowl, top with the grated egg, and garnish with blue cheese fritters.

Lobster Salad *with marinated melon and jalapeño oil*

Combine 12 cups water, the wine, black peppercorns, lemons, bay leaves, and thyme in a large stockpot and boil for 10 minutes. Reduce the heat to low and add the lobsters. Bring to a simmer and cook for 7 minutes. Remove the lobsters from the hot water and cool them in an ice bath. Extract the meat from the tails and claws and set aside.

To make the candied lemon zest, zest both lemons using a zester, creating long thin strips of yellow skin only (no white pith). In a small saucepot, boil the lemon zest for 2 minutes. Drain the liquid and repeat the operation twice to remove any bitterness. Drain the liquid for the final time and combine the blanched lemon zest, sugar, and 4 tablespoons water in the saucepot and cook slowly over low heat for 20 minutes, or until candied.

Peel the melons and cut them into 3-inch-long pieces. Place the pieces in a shallow baking dish. Combine the lime juice, coriander, Szechuan peppercorns, mint, olive oil, candied lemon zest, and salt and black pepper to taste in a mixing bowl and pour the mixture over the melons. Marinate the melons in the mixture in the refrigerator for 1 hour.

To make the jalapeño oil, combine the canola oil and jalapeños in a blender and process them until smooth. Add salt and refrigerate the oil until you are ready to use.

Cut the lobster tail meat into ½-inch rounds. Season the lobster with salt and black pepper and drizzle it with extra virgin olive oil and a little lime juice.

To serve, stack the melons decoratively on individual serving plates and arrange the lobster rounds around the plate. Top with the lobster claws. Drizzle the salad with jalapeño oil and a few drops of balsamic vinegar, and garnish with chopped chives and basil leaves.

LOBSTER
4 cups dry white wine
2 tablespoons black peppercorns
2 lemons, sliced
2 bay leaves
1 teaspoon dried thyme
2 (1½-pound) live lobsters

CANDIED LEMON ZEST
2 lemons
2 tablespoons sugar

MARINATED MELON
¼ small watermelon
½ cantaloupe
½ honeydew melon
Juice of 4 limes
1 tablespoon coriander seeds, cracked
1 teaspoon Szechuan peppercorns, cracked
2 tablespoons chopped mint
¼ cup extra virgin olive oil
Salt and black pepper

JALAPEÑO OIL
¼ cup canola oil
3 jalapeños, halved and seeded
½ tablespoon salt

Salt and black pepper
Extra virgin olive oil
Fresh lime juice
1 tablespoon aged balsamic vinegar
1 tablespoon chopped chives
Fresh basil leaves

Warm Potato Salad *with smoked salmon*

SERVES 4

1½ pounds fingerling potatoes
¼ cup sour cream
¼ cup whole grain mustard
½ clove garlic, chopped
Juice and zest of 1 lemon
1 tablespoon minced chives
Salt
Cracked black pepper
1 pound smoked salmon
1 tablespoon extra virgin olive oil
3½ tablespoons sliced red onion
1 tablespoon fresh dill

Boil the potatoes in a large saucepot over high heat for 20 minutes, or until they are cooked through. Remove from the heat, drain, and allow the potatoes to cool. Remove the skin and cut the potatoes into ¼-inch cubes. Set aside and keep warm.

In a small mixing bowl, combine the sour cream, mustard, garlic, lemon juice (reserve 1 teaspoon lemon juice for the salmon), chives, and a pinch of salt and black pepper to taste.

Slice the smoked salmon and drizzle with olive oil, lemon zest, and a touch of lemon juice.

To serve, spread a spoonful of the sour cream–mustard mixture in the middle of a round plate and top with a mound of warm potatoes. Arrange the sliced red onion and smoked salmon on top, and garnish with fresh dill and cracked black pepper before serving.

THE MANSION ON TURTLE CREEK

Crispy Fried Oysters and Spinach Salad
with bacon, blue cheese, and mushroom dressing

SERVES 4

Put the flour in a medium mixing bowl, season with salt and black pepper, and stir to combine. Beat the eggs in a separate mixing bowl. Pour the cornmeal into another medium mixing bowl and season with salt, black pepper, the cayenne pepper, and chopped parsley and stir to combine.

Place each oyster in the seasoned flour and shake off the excess. Dip the oyster in the egg bowl, then into the cornmeal mixture. Toss to coat and gently press the cornmeal mixture onto each oyster. Reserve the oysters on a paper towel for frying.

Combine the sliced onion and lemon juice in a mixing bowl and set aside.

In a sauté pan over medium heat, cook the bacon until it is almost crisp and the fat is rendered. Add ¼ cup olive oil, the shallots, and mushrooms and cook for 5 minutes, or until tender. Add salt and black pepper to taste. Add the vinegar and the onion-lemon juice mixture, and bring to a simmer. Continue to simmer for 3 minutes, then remove from the heat.

Heat the peanut oil to 360 degrees F in a 4-quart saucepan. Carefully fry the oysters, 6 at a time, for 4 to 5 minutes or until crisp. Drain on a paper towel.

Add the blue cheese to the warm mushroom and bacon mixture and stir briefly. In a large mixing bowl, combine the spinach and the prepared dressing and toss to coat.

Divide the salad among four salad plates, garnish with 3 of the oysters each, and serve.

3 cups all-purpose flour
Salt
Cracked black pepper
6 eggs, beaten
4 cups yellow cornmeal
½ teaspoon cayenne pepper
1 tablespoon chopped fresh parsley
12 Lady Chatterly Choice Oysters, opened, or any meaty Gulf oyster
1 red onion, sliced
Juice of 3 lemons
1½ pounds hickory smoked bacon, cut into ¼-inch dice
½ cup extra virgin olive oil
2 shallots, minced
1 pound cremini mushrooms, cleaned and sliced
¼ cup sherry vinegar
3 quarts peanut oil
8 ounces Maytag blue cheese, crumbled
2 (16-ounce) bags baby spinach, stemmed, washed, and dried

Paula Lambert / THE MOZZARELLA COMPANY

BLAME IT ON THE CAPRESE SALAD. Paula Lambert would never have opened her ground-breaking Mozzarella Company in 1982 in Dallas had it not been for that simplest of Italian salads. Those circles of creamy mozzarella so strikingly alternating with red tomatoes and flecked with fresh basil are a testament to symmetry, freshness, and minimalism. When Lambert fell in love with this unfussy luxury in the sixties, she was working at Cantine Giorgio Lungarotti, a now-famous winery in Torgiano, Italy, and the salad was a recent culinary development. Made "in the style of Capri," the red-green-and-white taste teaser had become a sensation after it was served to Egypt's jet-setting King Farouk on a visit to Capri in the fifties.

It wasn't King Farouk but the fresh mozzarella—unheard of in Texas in the sixties—that captivated Lambert's imagination. Spongy and oozing with milky goodness, the cheese was a revelation to the recent college graduate. Lambert missed it every time she had to return home to the States. "My goal became to produce mozzarella that I would sell as soon as it was made, just like they did in Italy," says Lambert. She studied with Italian cheesemakers and when confident in her skills, returned to Texas and leased a building in 1982 in the up-and-coming Deep Ellum district of Dallas.

Lambert immediately began to evangelize about her obsession. She knocked on the back door of the best restaurant in town. "Our first month in business," she says, "I went to the Mansion." Tomato and mozzarella salad was already on the menu there, but the cheese wasn't handmade, nor was it fresh. Star chef Wolfgang Puck was the Mansion's menu consultant and recognized that Lambert's notions were on the sharpest of cutting edges. Puck insisted this is what Dallas needed—local food, produced locally.

Paula Lambert happened to be at the right place at the right time. The novice cheesemaker had unknowingly tapped into the food movement started by California chef Alice Waters, who used her restaurant Chez Panisse as a forum to demonstrate the wonders of organic, locally grown and produced food. The idea was novel and exciting—and once Lambert's customers tasted her mozzarella made just a few miles from the Mansion, the definition of concepts like "fresh" and "delicious" changed forever. "It was a great period," Lambert recalls.

Today Lambert is still in the same Deep Ellum factory (it's a lot more cramped for space), and she's expanded her offerings to include other cheeses such as goat cheese. You can tell the white aromatic delicacy is from Texas: Instead of the smack of citrusy attitude this cheese is known for, here the drier grasses that goats nibble on evoke a toastier, peppery flavor. Chefs at the Mansion have showcased the cheese on the restaurant's menu. The roasted beet and goat cheese salad is the yin and yang of color and texture, a scintillating challenge from robust root vegetable to nuanced cheese. For dessert, Paula Lambert's goat cheese cheesecake levitates above and beyond the popular conception of this dessert, a provocative invitation that Paula Lambert's love affair with handmade cheese must be ours, too.

Paula Lambert's Roasted Beet and Goat Cheese Salad

SERVES 4

6 baseball-sized red beets
5 whole cloves garlic
2 sprigs fresh thyme
1 tablespoon whole black peppercorns
2 bay leaves
Extra virgin olive oil
Sea salt
Chianti vinegar or other red wine
  vinegar
Black pepper
8 ounces Paula Lambert's premium
  goat cheese
¼ cup chopped chives
2 tablespoons crème fraîche
Mixed micro greens

RED BEET DRESSING
(Yields 2 cups)
½ pound cooked red beet trimmings
1 cup chicken stock
½ cup Chianti vinegar or other red
  wine vinegar
½ pint fresh raspberries
½ cup extra virgin olive oil
Salt and black pepper

Preheat the oven to 350 degrees F. Place the beets in a metal baking pan and pour 1 cup of water in the bottom of the pan. Add the garlic, thyme, peppercorns, and bay leaves.

Drizzle the beets with olive oil and sprinkle with sea salt. Cover the pan tightly with aluminum foil and bake for 3 hours, or until the beets are tender. Check for doneness by sticking a knife tip into a beet—the knife should easily pierce the beet. When done, drain the liquid from the pan and allow the beets to cool at room temperature.

When cool, use a Japanese mandoline to slice the beets into ⅛-inch slices. Cut the beet slices into uniform circles with a 2½-inch round cookie or biscuit cutter, reserving the trimmings. Arrange the beet circles on a parchment-lined baking sheet and drizzle with olive oil and red wine vinegar, and season with salt and pepper. Cover with plastic wrap and refrigerate for 1 hour.

To make the dressing, put the beet trimmings, chicken stock, vinegar, and raspberries in a medium saucepan over medium heat. Bring the mixture to a boil, reduce the heat, and simmer for 10 minutes. Remove from the heat and puree the mixture in a blender. Pass the mixture through a fine conical strainer, discard the solids, and return the liquid to the saucepan. Cook over low heat until the mixture reduces and becomes syrupy enough to coat the back of a spoon. Pour the hot mixture into a mixing bowl set over an ice bath. As the dressing cools, slowly whisk in the olive oil until it is fully incorporated. Season with salt and pepper and refrigerate the dressing until you are ready to serve. Leftover dressing can be refrigerated for two weeks.

To assemble the salad, combine the goat cheese, chopped chives, crème fraîche, salt, and pepper in a medium mixing bowl and whisk to a creamy consistency. Transfer the mixture to a pastry bag. Pipe the cheese onto half of the beet rounds and top with the other half of the rounds to form sandwiches. Drizzle again with olive oil, salt, and pepper, and a few splashes of Chianti vinegar.

To serve, spoon three circles of the beet dressing in a triangle on each of four chilled plates. These circles should be a little bigger than the sandwiches. Place a beet sandwich on each dressing circle, pushing down slightly so they don't slide. Drizzle each sandwich with extra virgin olive oil, season with sea salt, and garnish with micro greens.

Mansion Salad *with fresh herb vinaigrette and cheese croutons*

To make the vinaigrette, combine the shallot, garlic, herbs, and vinegars in a small bowl. Whisk in the oils. Season to taste with the lemon juice and salt and whisk well. Set aside.

To make the croutons, preheat the oven to 375 degrees F. Place the bread slices on a baking sheet and toast for 4 minutes, or until the bread begins to brown, then turn and toast for another 4 minutes to brown both sides evenly. Preheat the broiler.

In a food processor, blend the goat cheese, cheddar cheese, Brie, and cream until smooth. Mix in the salt and cayenne pepper to taste. Spread a small amount of the cheese mixture on each toast slice. Place under the broiler just long enough to melt the cheese. Set aside and keep warm.

To assemble the salad, combine all the lettuces in a large mixing bowl with the fresh herb vinaigrette and toss to coat. To serve, place two endive leaves on a chilled salad plate and top with a generous portion of the salad. Garnish each serving with tomatoes and a warm cheese crouton and serve immediately.

FRESH HERB VINAIGRETTE
1 large shallot, minced
1 large clove garlic, minced
1 teaspoon minced basil
1 teaspoon minced thyme
1 teaspoon minced parsley
1 teaspoon minced tarragon
1 teaspoon minced chives
1½ tablespoons white wine vinegar
1 teaspoon balsamic vinegar
4 tablespoons peanut oil
1 tablespoon extra virgin olive oil
Juice of ½ lemon
Salt

CHEESE CROUTONS
8 (½-inch-thick) slices French baguette
2 ounces fresh goat cheese
2 ounces white cheddar cheese
2 ounces Brie
2 tablespoons heavy cream
Salt
Cayenne pepper

SALAD
1 small head Boston or Bibb lettuce, washed and chopped
1 small head red oak lettuce or radicchio, washed and chopped
2 bundles mâche lettuce, washed and chopped
1 head baby white chicory, washed and chopped
1 head Belgian endive, washed, leaves separated
4 red baby pear tomatoes
4 yellow baby pear tomatoes

Fish & Shellfish

Louisiana Crawfish Stew

Seared Scallops

Roasted Monkfish

Seared Scallops and Fried Sardine Samosa

Grilled Tuna

Salmon with Gala Apple

Chorizo-Crusted Halibut

Grilled Gulf Red Snapper

Grilled Swordfish

Crispy Salted Cod and Potato Napoleon

Broiled Gulf Prawns

Grilled Lobster

Seared Gulf Red Snapper

Louisiana Crawfish Stew
with red mole and lime

SERVES 4

RED MOLE

1 cup peanut oil
3 dried pasilla chiles
1 dried ancho chile
2 dried guajillo chiles
2 cloves garlic, crushed
1 onion, sliced
½ teaspoon dried thyme
1 bay leaf
½ teaspoon dried marjoram
½ teaspoon ground cumin
½ tablespoon ground cinnamon
½ teaspoon ground black pepper
2 tablespoons sesame seeds, toasted
¼ teaspoon ground cloves
¼ cup chopped bitter dark chocolate
4 cups chicken stock
3 tablespoons bread crumbs
Salt

CRAWFISH STEWING LIQUID

½ medium onion
1 carrot, halved
1 lemon, sliced
2 bay leaves
1 teaspoon salt
2 tablespoons black peppercorns
6 pounds live crawfish

STEW

4 cloves garlic
½ medium onion, diced
1 carrot, diced
3 tablespoons extra virgin olive oil
2 cups dried black beans, soaked in
   water overnight
4 cups chicken stock
Salt and black pepper
1 tablespoon unsalted butter
2 limes, cut into wedges, for garnish
1 tablespoon chopped cilantro,
   for garnish

To make the mole, heat the peanut oil in a large cast-iron pot over high heat. Do not allow the oil to smoke. Fry the chiles in three batches for 20 to 30 seconds, turning them constantly. The chiles should turn bright red. Place the chiles in a mixing bowl, add enough hot water to cover, and soak for 30 minutes.

Discard half the oil in the pot and return the pot to medium heat. Add the garlic, onion, thyme, bay leaf, and marjoram and cook for 10 minutes. Add the cumin, cinnamon, black pepper, toasted sesame seeds, and cloves and cook for 6 more minutes.

When the chiles are done soaking, seed them, and puree using a blender, adding a little soaking water as needed to achieve a paste consistency. Add the chile paste to the cast-iron pot and cook for 5 minutes more. Add the chocolate, stirring until melted, and add the chicken stock. Reduce the heat to low and cook for 30 minutes. Add the bread crumbs and puree the sauce in a blender until smooth. Season with salt to taste. Keep warm until ready to serve, or store, covered, in the freezer for up to four weeks.

Combine 10 quarts water, the onion, carrot, lemon slices, bay leaves, salt, and black peppercorns in a large stockpot and boil for 10 minutes. Add the crawfish and cook for 5 minutes. Remove the crawfish and spread them on a baking sheet to cool. When cool, extract the tail meat and set it aside.

In a separate stockpot, cook the garlic, onion, and carrot in the olive oil for 5 minutes over medium heat. Drain the black beans and add them to the pot. Add just enough chicken stock to cover the beans and cook for 20 minutes. Season with a pinch of salt and black pepper. There should be almost no liquid left in the beans. Stir in the butter.

To serve, scoop the beans into a bowl and top with the crawfish tails. Pour the mole around the tails and garnish the dish with fresh cilantro and lime wedges.

THE MANSION ON TURTLE CREEK

Seared Scallops *with braised savoy cabbage*

SERVES 4

GINGER DRESSING
1 tablespoon grated fresh ginger
1 teaspoon chopped garlic
1 tablespoon rice vinegar
2 tablespoons extra virgin olive oil
1 teaspoon chile flakes
3 scallions, thinly sliced

SOY GLAZE
½ cup mirin (Japanese rice wine,
    found in Asian markets)
1 cup sweet soy sauce
1 tablespoon chopped fresh ginger
3 cloves garlic, chopped
1 tablespoon green peppercorns

CABBAGE
1 tablespoon unsalted butter
2 cloves garlic, crushed
1 large head green savoy cabbage,
    cut in large cubes (may substitute
    green cabbage)
1 cup chicken stock
Salt and black pepper

SCALLOPS
12 large scallops
Salt and black pepper
1 tablespoon unsalted butter
1 tablespoon extra virgin olive oil

To make the ginger dressing, whisk together the ginger, garlic, vinegar, extra virgin olive oil, chile flakes, and scallions in a mixing bowl. Cover and refrigerate the dressing for 20 minutes before serving.

To make the glaze for the cabbage, cook the mirin in a small saucepot over medium heat for 10 minutes, stirring occasionally, until it reduces and thickens. Add the soy sauce and simmer for 5 minutes. Remove the pot from the heat and add the ginger, garlic, and green peppercorns. Set the glaze aside and allow it to cool.

Heat the butter in a large sauté pan over high heat and cook the garlic for 2 minutes. Add the cabbage and cook for 10 minutes, stirring occasionally, until the cabbage begins to caramelize. Add the chicken stock and continue cooking for 5 minutes more, or until the stock has evaporated. Season with a pinch of salt and black pepper, set aside, and keep warm.

Season the scallops with salt and pepper on both sides. In a nonstick frying pan over high heat, add 1 tablespoon extra virgin olive oil and 1 tablespoon butter. Sear the scallops for 3 minutes on each side.

To serve, place the cabbage on a large plate and arrange the scallops around. With a brush, paint the scallops with the soy glaze. Drizzle the ginger dressing over the top and around the plate.

Roasted Monkfish *with short rib hash*

Serves 4

Preheat the oven to 300 degrees F. Season the short ribs with salt and pepper. In a sauté pan over high heat, sear the beef in the canola oil on both sides for 3 minutes, or until the ribs have a nice crust.

In a large, ovenproof braising pan big enough for the beef, sauté the vegetables in the extra virgin olive oil over high heat for 7 minutes, stirring often. Add the seared beef, cover with the red wine and vinegar, and add the bay leaf and thyme. Cover the pan and bake in the oven for 3 hours.

Remove the ribs from the oven. Strain the cooking liquid into a sauté pan and discard the vegetables. Reduce the cooking liquid to a sauce consistency. Add 1 tablespoon of butter, and season with salt and pepper. Shred the short ribs and warm them up in the sauce. Set aside and keep the short ribs warm until ready to serve.

Rinse the potatoes and dry them on a paper towel. Heat 3 inches of vegetable oil in a saucepot over medium heat. Fry the potatoes for 5 minutes, or until golden brown. Reserve them on a paper towel and season with salt.

To prepare the monkfish, preheat the oven to 375 degrees F. Season the fish with salt and pepper. Heat an ovenproof sauté pan with 2 tablespoons of the extra virgin olive oil over high heat. Sear the fish for 4 minutes, or until golden brown on all sides. Add the butter, garlic, and thyme and transfer the fish to the oven to cook for 5 minutes, basting often to keep the fish moist. Remove from the oven and allow the fish to rest for 5 minutes before slicing into ½-inch pieces.

Sauté the mushrooms in 1 tablespoon extra virgin olive oil in a sauté pan over high heat for 5 minutes. Season the mushrooms with salt and pepper. Place the short ribs, crispy potatoes, and mushrooms in four deep plates. Arrange the monkfish on top and garnish with sea salt and chopped parsley to serve.

Short Ribs

2 pounds beef short ribs, uncut
Salt and black pepper
1 tablespoon canola oil
2 carrots, peeled and sliced
½ onion, peeled and sliced
3 cloves garlic, peeled
2 stalks celery, chopped
½ cup white mushrooms, halved
2 tablespoons extra virgin olive oil
6 cups red wine
2 tablespoons red wine vinegar
1 bay leaf
1 teaspoon fresh thyme
1 tablespoon unsalted butter

Potatoes and Monkfish

2 Idaho potatoes, peeled and diced
   into ⅓-inch cubes
Vegetable oil
Salt
1½ pounds monkfish loin, cleaned
Black pepper
3 tablespoons extra virgin olive oil
1 tablespoon unsalted butter
1 clove garlic, crushed
1 sprig fresh thyme
1 cup shiitake mushrooms, cleaned
   and stemmed
1 tablespoon chopped Italian parsley

Seared Scallops and Fried Sardine Samosa

SERVES 4

4 cups grapeseed oil
1 daikon radish, peeled and cut into
    2 x 1-inch rounds
8 (U10) sea scallops
6 tablespoons unsalted butter,
    softened
4 whole fresh sardines, gutted and
    cleaned
2 cups flour
Salt and black pepper
4 eggs, beaten
2 cups panko (Japanese bread crumbs)
2 tablespoons extra virgin olive oil
Fleur de sel

TOMATO CHUTNEY
(page 160)

Chives for garnish (optional)

In a medium sauté pan over medium heat, add a little grapeseed oil and heat until the oil begins to shimmer. Sear each daikon round until both sides are golden brown. Set aside on a paper towel to dry.

Using a brush, coat one side of the scallops with the softened butter. Heat ¼ cup grapeseed oil in an iron skillet over medium heat until the oil is smoking. Add the scallops to the pan, buttered-side down, and cook for 2 to 3 minutes, checking for a golden brown sear. Flip the scallops over and drain the oil from the pan. Return the pan to the heat, add 2 tablespoons butter to the pan, and baste the scallops with the butter using a spoon for 2 minutes, or until they are fully cooked. Transfer the scallops to a paper towel to dry.

Pour the flour into a shallow bowl and season with salt and pepper. Hold a sardine by the tail and dredge it in the flour. Shake off the excess, and dip the sardine in the beaten egg. Still holding the tail, press the panko bread crumbs onto the sardine to coat. Repeat the process with the remaining sardines and set them aside on a plate. Heat 3 cups grapeseed oil to 360 degrees F in a saucepan and fry the sardines for 3 minutes, or until golden brown. Drain them on a paper towel and set aside.

Place two scallops on each plate and season with a little sea salt and black pepper. Place a daikon round on each plate, and top the daikon with a sardine. Drizzle with tomato chutney and a little extra virgin olive oil and garnish with chives.

Grilled Tuna *with eggplant, fried pearl onions, and Texas green tomato chutney*

SERVES 4

FRIED PEARL ONIONS

8 pearl onions, peeled and thinly
    sliced on a Japanese mandoline
2 tablespoons all-purpose flour
Vegetable oil
Salt

TOMATO CHUTNEY

3 tablespoons corn syrup
1 pound green tomatoes, cubed
½ small white onion, cubed
1 teaspoon cumin seeds
Juice of 1 lemon
1 bay leaf

CILANTRO PESTO

1 cup cilantro
2 cloves garlic
6 mint leaves
3 tablespoons extra virgin olive oil
1 tablespoon toasted pine nuts
Juice of 1 lemon
Salt

TUNA

1 tablespoon ketchup
1 tablespoon soy sauce
1 clove garlic, crushed
5 drops Tabasco sauce
1 teaspoon rice vinegar
1 ½ pounds Ahi tuna, cut into
    four 1-inch pieces

1 pound Japanese eggplant,
    sliced ½-inch thick
Salt
2 tablespoons extra virgin olive oil

Coat the onion rings in the all-purpose flour. Fill a saucepot with 2 inches of vegetable oil and fry the onion rings over medium heat for 3 minutes, or until golden brown. Drain them on a paper towel, season with salt, and set aside.

To make the chutney, cook the corn syrup in a braising pan over high heat until it is lightly caramelized. Add the tomatoes, onion, cumin seeds, lemon juice, and bay leaf. Reduce the heat to medium and cook for 20 minutes, or until the chutney has the consistency of jam. Adjust the seasoning and set the chutney aside at room temperature.

To make the cilantro pesto, combine the cilantro, garlic, mint, extra virgin olive oil, pine nuts, and lemon juice in a blender. Process the mixture until it becomes an oily paste. Season with salt, cover, and refrigerate until you are ready to serve.

To make the tuna, combine the ketchup, soy sauce, garlic, Tabasco, and rice vinegar in a mixing bowl. Marinate the tuna steak in this mixture for 10 minutes in the refrigerator.

Season the eggplant with salt, wrap in plastic wrap, and set aside for 10 minutes to draw the moisture out of the eggplant. Remove the plastic, dry the eggplant on a paper towel, and drizzle with extra virgin olive oil. Grill the eggplant for 3 minutes on each side, then keep warm until ready to serve.

Grill the tuna for 2 minutes on both sides to achieve a rare temperature. Serve the tuna on a large plate with a few slices of grilled eggplant and a spoonful of the green tomato chutney. Garnish with the cilantro pesto and a few fried onions on top.

Salmon with Gala Apple
and celery-horseradish puree

To make the puree, place the celeriac in a 3-quart saucepot. Cover the celeriac with the milk and 1 cup water. Season with salt and bring to a boil. Reduce the heat and cover the mixture with a disc of parchment paper. Cook for 25 minutes, or until the celeriac softens. Drain the mixture in a conical strainer and reserve 1 cup of the hot milk. Place the celeriac in a blender, add the reserved milk, and process the mixture until smooth. Adjust the seasoning if needed, add the horseradish, and reserve the puree in the warm saucepot.

In a separate saucepot over medium heat, sauté the shallots and carrot with 1 tablespoon of extra virgin olive oil for 2 minutes. Add the red wine and port. Cook for 25 minutes over low heat. Using an immersion blender, blend the mixture to obtain a silky sauce. Pass the sauce through a conical strainer and back into the saucepot. Season with salt and pepper and keep warm until ready to serve.

In a sauté pan over high heat, sauté the apples in 1 tablespoon of the butter for 3 minutes on each side, or until they start to caramelize. Set aside and keep warm.

Season the salmon with salt, pepper, and ancho chile powder. In a sauté pan over medium heat, sear the salmon for 4 minutes on each side for a medium temperature.

Just before serving, add 1 tablespoon of butter to the celeriac puree and whisk to combine.

Spread a spoonful of the celeriac puree on each plate and place the salmon next to it. Arrange the caramelized apple around the salmon and finish with the red wine sauce to serve.

CELERY–HORSERADISH PUREE
1 large celeriac (celery root), peeled and diced
4 cups milk
Salt
2 tablespoons shredded fresh horseradish

RED WINE SAUCE
2 shallots, sliced
½ carrot, peeled and sliced
1 tablespoon extra virgin olive oil
4 cups merlot
½ cup red port
Salt and black pepper

2 Gala apples, peeled, cored, and sliced into thin wedges
2 tablespoons unsalted butter
1 ½ pounds salmon fillet, skin removed, cut into four equal pieces
Salt and black pepper
1 tablespoon ancho chile powder

Chorizo-Crusted Halibut *with white bean puree and stuffed piquillo peppers*

SERVES 4

To make the bean puree, in a saucepot over medium heat, add the extra virgin olive oil, diced onion, carrot, and garlic. Sauté the vegetables for 3 minutes. Drain the beans and add to them to the pot. Cook for 3 minutes more and cover the vegetables with chicken stock. Add the bay leaf and thyme and cook, covered, for 30 minutes. Remove the pot from the heat and allow the liquid to cool. Strain the cooking liquid, reserving 1 cup to make the sauce later. Place the rest of the cooking liquid in a blender with the beans and blend until a puree consistency is achieved. Season with salt and pepper and set aside.

To make the peppers, in a sauté pan over medium heat, roast the fennel, onion, and garlic for 10 minutes. Cover the vegetables with 2 cups chicken stock and cook for 10 minutes, or until the stock has evaporated. The mixture should be the consistency of marmalade. Season with salt and pepper and set aside.

Preheat the oven to 375 degrees F. Stuff the piquillo peppers with the fennel mixture. Place the stuffed peppers in a baking dish, drizzle with extra virgin olive oil, and pour 3 tablespoons of chicken stock in the dish with ½ tablespoon butter. Cover the dish with foil and cook for 20 minutes. Remove the peppers from the oven and keep them warm until you are ready to serve.

To make the sauce, boil the Roma tomatoes in 4 cups of water in a saucepot for 10 seconds. Transfer them to an ice bath to cool. Remove the skins, then halve and seed the tomatoes before dicing them into ¼-inch cubes. Reserve the tomatoes in a mixing bowl. Reheat the 1 cup reserved white bean cooking liquid in a saucepot over medium-high heat, and reduce the liquid by half. Add 1 tablespoon of the extra virgin olive oil, the diced tomato, chopped parsley, and sherry vinegar and heat through. Adjust the seasoning as desired and set aside.

Combine the mustard with the harissa paste or Tabasco in a small bowl and set aside. In a separate bowl, mix the diced chorizo with the bread crumbs. Add 2 tablespoons extra virgin olive oil and season with salt and pepper.

Season the halibut with salt and pepper. Sear the fish in 1 tablespoon extra virgin olive oil in a sauté pan over high heat, cooking for 4 minutes on both sides. Brush the fish with the mustard mixture, then top it with the chorizo crust.

Pour the hot bean puree onto the bottoms of four large plates. Top the puree with the fish and one roasted piquillo. Garnish with the tomato sauce and serve.

WHITE BEAN PUREE
2 tablespoons extra virgin olive oil
½ medium white onion, peeled and diced
1 carrot, peeled and halved
1 clove garlic, crushed
1 cup dried cannellini beans, soaked overnight in 4 cups cold water
4 cups chicken stock
1 bay leaf
1 sprig fresh thyme
Salt and black pepper

STUFFED PIQUILLO PEPPERS
2 bulbs fennel, stemmed and sliced
½ medium white onion, sliced
1 clove garlic, crushed
2 cups plus 3 tablespoons chicken stock
Salt and black pepper
4 canned piquillo peppers
Extra virgin olive oil
½ tablespoon unsalted butter

SAUCE
2 Roma tomatoes
1 tablespoon extra virgin olive oil
2 tablespoons chopped Italian parsley
½ tablespoon sherry vinegar

CHORIZO-CRUSTED HALIBUT
2 tablespoons Dijon mustard
1 teaspoon harissa paste (or a few drops of Tabasco sauce)
½ cup diced dry Spanish chorizo
4 tablespoons bread crumbs
3 tablespoons extra virgin olive oil
Salt and black pepper
1½ pounds halibut fillet, cleaned and cut into 6-ounce pieces

Clockwise fron top left:
Chipotle
Pasilla
De Arbol
Ancho
Guajillo
Cascabel, New Mexico

Clockwise fron top left:
Bell Pepper
Jalapeño
Poblano
Annaheim
Serrano
Habanero (center)

Grilled Gulf Red Snapper *with tomatillo–serrano chile vinaigrette and cornbread oysters*

TOMATILLO–SERRANO CHILE VINAIGRETTE

1 pound tomatillos, husks removed, diced
½ cup diced jicama
½ cup diced mango
2 tablespoons diced red bell pepper
2 tablespoons diced yellow bell pepper
2 serrano chiles, seeded and finely chopped
1 cup peanut oil
2 tablespoons extra virgin olive oil
¼ cup white wine vinegar
2 tablespoons balsamic vinegar
Juice of ½ lime
2 teaspoons fresh lemon juice
2 tablespoons chopped cilantro
1 clove garlic, minced
Salt

CORNBREAD OYSTERS

3 cups peanut oil
1½ cups yellow cornmeal
½ cup flour
2 teaspoons baking powder
1 teaspoon salt
2 extra large eggs, lightly beaten
¼ cup bacon grease, melted
2 cups milk
2 tablespoons fresh oyster liquor, or as needed
12 fresh oysters, shucked

GRILLED GULF RED SNAPPER

4 (7-ounce) red snapper fillets, skin removed on one side
3 tablespoons peanut oil
Salt and black pepper

To make the vinaigrette, combine the tomatillos, jicama, mango, red and yellow peppers, and serrano chiles in a medium bowl. In a separate bowl, combine the peanut and olive oils, vinegars, and lime and lemon juices. Blend in the cilantro, garlic, and salt to taste. Pour the oil mixture over the tomatillo mixture and stir to blend. Cover and set aside at room temperature. This can be prepared several hours ahead of time.

Using a deep-sided pot, heat the oil to 375 degrees F. Lightly stir together the cornmeal, flour, baking powder, and salt in a large mixing bowl. Add the eggs, bacon grease, and milk. Add just enough oyster liquor (about 2 tablespoons) to make the mixture the consistency of cornbread batter. Stir the batter until smooth. If the batter is too thick, add a bit more milk. If it is too thin, add a bit more cornmeal. (Excess batter can be refrigerated, tightly covered, for up to three days and may be used for breading vegetables and other fish.)

Dip each oyster into the batter and carefully lower the oyster into the hot oil. Do not crowd the pot. Add just enough oysters to the oil to form a single layer without touching one another. Fry the oysters, turning, until they are golden brown on both sides. Remove them from the oil and drain on a paper towel. The oysters may be fried ahead of time and kept warm while grilling the snapper.

Prepare the fire for grilling. Make sure the grates are clean and lightly rub them with oil just before placing the fish on the grill.

Dip the fillets in 3 tablespoons peanut oil and place them on the preheated grill, skin-side up. Season the skin side with salt and pepper to taste. Grill the snapper for about 2 minutes, just long enough to create grill marks on one side. Turn the fillets and season them lightly with salt and pepper. Cook for another 2 minutes, or just until the fish feels firm. Do not overcook. The fish should be very moist.

To serve, ladle the vinaigrette over the bottom of each of four dinner plates. Place a red snapper fillet in the middle of each plate. Arrange three oysters in a triangle pattern at even intervals near the rim of each plate.

Grilled Swordfish *with pineapple–red chile salsa*

SERVES 6

PINEAPPLE–RED CHILE SALSA

½ very ripe pineapple, peeled, cored, and chopped
½ mango or papaya, peeled, pitted (or seeded), and chopped
½ red bell pepper, chopped
½ yellow bell pepper, chopped
¼ jicama, chopped
½ tablespoon grated fresh ginger
1 clove garlic, minced
1 serrano chile, seeded and minced
2 dried cayenne chiles, seeded and minced (or ⅛ teaspoon ground cayenne pepper)
2 teaspoons minced cilantro
2 teaspoons minced basil
2 teaspoons minced mint
1 tablespoon white wine vinegar
1 tablespoon sweet rice vinegar
1 teaspoon soy sauce
1 teaspoon sesame oil
Salt
Juice of 1 lime

GRILLED SWORDFISH

6 (7-ounce) swordfish steaks, trimmed of fat, skin, and dark membrane
3 tablespoons sesame oil
Salt

To make the salsa, process the pineapple, mango, bell peppers, jicama, ginger, garlic, and serrano and cayenne chiles in a food processor to make medium-sized chunks. Be careful to not puree the mixture. In a medium-sized mixing bowl, combine the fruits and vegetables with their juices and the herbs, vinegars, soy sauce, oil, and salt and lime juice to taste. Let macerate for 2 hours before serving at room temperature.

Preheat the grill. Make sure the grates are clean, and rub them with vegetable oil before placing the fish on the grill. Brush the fish steaks with 3 tablespoons sesame oil and season to taste with salt.

Place the steaks on the preheated grill and cook for 2 minutes, or just long enough to create grill marks on one side. Turn the fish and cook for 2 minutes more, or until the fish is firm. Allow no more than 5 minutes of total cooking time for each ½ inch of thickness at the thickest part of the fish. Do not overcook. The fish should be moist.

To serve, ladle the salsa over the bottom of each of six warm dinner plates. Place the swordfish steaks in the center and serve immediately.

Crispy Salted Cod and Potato Napoleon

SERVES 4

Rub the cod fillet with the sea salt. Set the fish aside to sit for 20 minutes, allowing the fish to cure.

Preheat the oven to 375 degrees F. Rinse the potato slices in cold water and dry them on a paper towel. Lay them out on parchment-lined sheet pan. Brush them with canola oil and season with salt, pepper, and sweet paprika. Place another sheet of parchment paper over the top. Cook them in the oven for 20 minutes, or until golden brown. Remove the potatoes from the oven and set them aside on paper towels to dry.

Rinse the fish in cold water to remove the salt. Set it on a paper towel to dry, season with cayenne pepper, and drizzle with extra virgin olive oil. Spread the garlic over the fish, place it in a baking dish, and bake in the oven for 15 minutes.

To make the tomato lemon sauce, combine the tomatoes, lemon, capers, parsley, chives, extra virgin olive oil, balsamic vinegar, salt, and pepper in a mixing bowl. Cover and allow the sauce to marinate in the refrigerator for 10 minutes.

Flake the fish into pieces. On a round serving plate, build a four-layer Napoleon layering the pieces of cooked fish and the crispy potatoes, starting with a layer of the potatoes and ending with the fish on top. Spoon the lemon-tomato sauce over the plate, and garnish with the arugula.

1½ pounds (1-inch-thick) cod fillets, skin removed
½ cup coarse sea salt
3 large Idaho potatoes, thinly sliced on a Japanese mandoline
Canola oil
Salt and black pepper
1 tablespoon sweet paprika
½ cup extra virgin olive oil
½ tablespoon cayenne pepper
2 cloves garlic, crushed

TOMATO LEMON SAUCE
1 cup teardrop tomatoes, halved
2 lemons, peeled and segmented
½ tablespoon capers
½ tablespoon chopped Italian parsley
1 tablespoon chopped chives
4 tablespoons extra virgin olive oil
2 tablespoons aged balsamic vinegar
Salt and black pepper

1 cup arugula, for garnish

Broiled Gulf Prawns *with corn and sweet pepper relish*

SERVES 4

In a sauté pan big enough for the corn, melt the butter over medium heat. Add the corn and sauté for about 10 minutes, or until the kernels are tender. Transfer the corn to a parchment-lined sheet tray and cool. When the corn has cooled, transfer it to a medium mixing bowl. Add the red onion, jalapeños, piquillo peppers, cilantro, espelette, lime juice, and sherry vinegar. Season with salt and pepper to taste and set aside.

Preheat the grill to medium heat. Clean and oil the grates. In a large mixing bowl, combine the extra virgin olive oil, espellete, lemon juice, chives, salt, and a few turns of black pepper and mix well. Add the prawns and toss to coat. Add more oil if the prawns seem too dry. Grill the prawns on one side for 2 to 3 minutes, and then flip over. Grill for an additional 2 to 3 minutes, or until cooked through.

Place the corn relish in the middle of four large, oval plates. Place five prawns on each plate and garnish with cilantro sprigs and lime wedges to serve.

CORN AND SWEET PEPPER RELISH

10 ears fresh corn, kernels removed from the cob
4 tablespoons unsalted butter
1 red onion, finely diced
3 jalapeños, finely diced
5 canned piquillo peppers, diced
2 tablespoons chopped cilantro, plus sprigs for garnish
1 teaspoon espelette (may substitute ½ teaspoon cayenne pepper)
Juice of 2 limes
1 tablespoon sherry vinegar
Salt and black pepper

5 tablespoons extra virgin olive oil
2 teaspoons espelette (may substitute ½ teaspoon cayenne pepper)
Juice of 1 lemon
1 tablespoon chopped chives
Salt
Black pepper
20 (U10) Texas Gulf Prawns, heads on, peeled and deveined
Lime wedges

This is as close to barbecue as the Mansion kitchen gets.

Grilled Lobster *with fresh herbs, ancho chile butter, and crushed potato*

SERVES 4

ANCHO CHILE BUTTER
2 fresh jalapeños
2 cups (4 sticks) unsalted butter, softened
Juice of 3 lemons
3 tablespoons ancho chile powder
1 tablespoon chopped cilantro
Salt and black pepper

CRUSHED POTATOES
1 pound Yukon gold potatoes
3 tablespoons extra virgin olive oil
Salt and black pepper
1 tablespoon chopped chives

LOBSTER
4 (1½-pound) live lobsters
Extra virgin olive oil
1 tablespoon chopped chervil
1 tablespoon chopped Italian parsley
2 limes

To make the butter, grill the jalapeños for 10 minutes over medium-high heat. Allow them to cool, then remove and discard the skin and seeds, dice, and set aside. In a mixing bowl, combine the butter, lemon juice, ancho chile, chopped cilantro, and diced jalapeño. Mix well with a spoon, season with salt and pepper, and set aside.

Boil the potatoes in salted water for 25 minutes, or until soft. Drain and skin the potatoes, then mash them with a fork in a large mixing bowl. Add 3 tablespoons extra virgin olive oil, salt, pepper, and chives. Set aside and keep warm.

In a large stockpot filled with water, boil the lobsters for 2 minutes. Remove the lobsters from the water, halve them, and cool them on a baking sheet. Drizzle the tails and claws with extra virgin olive oil and grill them over medium heat, flesh-side down, for 4 minutes. When the lobster is lukewarm, coat the tails generously with the ancho chile butter. Place the tails and claws in a baking dish and broil them for 4 minutes.

Serve the lobster family-style on a large platter. Arrange the fresh herbs on top, zest the limes over the herbs, and serve the crushed potatoes on the side.

FARMERS ARE BORN OPTIMISTS. In order to succeed at what they do, a farmer has to dream big, plant with abandon, and ignore warnings from *The Farmers' Almanac*. Rocco Tassione grew up in the suburban wilds of Hurst, Texas, one of the mid-cities between Dallas and Fort Worth. As a teenager he longed to be at the hilly spread his father had bought near Stephenville, 90 miles west of Fort Worth. There Rocky and his friends would hunt, pitch a tent and camp, or just sit around a campfire and daydream. "I wanted to live out there," he says, "but I couldn't figure out how to make a living." Meanwhile, his country neighbors knew to bring their ailing plants to Tassione, who'd pamper them and nurse them back to health. And after he grew up, that was the clue that set the restless manager of dry cleaning businesses onto a new career path.

After Tassione got married, he had a willing accomplice in his wife, Celeste, a fellow foodie. "Our hobby," says Celeste, "was to go out to eat." So when Rocky woke up one morning in 1991 with an epiphany— "Why don't we farm for a living?"—Celeste grabbed a pen and paper and drew up a business plan. For the next three years Tassione took classes and attended seminars. He narrowed his farming goal to hydroponics, a method of growing plants, developed in the 19th century, that capitalized on a big discovery—that plants don't need soil in order to grow. In the hydroponic world, water is like heaven for plants, a place they go and live a better life. And hydroponics solved a lot of problems farmers always face: lashing storms and vicious tornados (plants are safe and sound in the greenhouses), attack by pests, soil reluctant to offer up its nutrients, and terrain not conducive to farming.

In 1995, it was official: The Tassiones traded their favorite hobby—eating—for their favorite job. With the conversion of a two-car garage to a growing room, complete with Mylar-lined walls and growing lights, the 150 acres near Stephenville became Tassione Farms. And a place that wasn't especially well suited to growing crops is today a fruitful wonderland aglow with thirteen 30 x 100-foot plastic-roofed greenhouses harboring the prettiest herbs and vegetables you've ever seen.

The Tassiones specialize in baby versions of vegetables, and not solely because of the cuteness factor. "The taste is sweet," rave chefs at the Mansion, "and incredible."

At Tassione Farms there are 20,000 baby head lettuces; four varieties of carrots—Purple Haze, Satin (a white one) Atomic Red, and an unnamed one that's yellow; tender bite-size collard greens; Tuscan kale; Bright Light chard; red Komatsuna microgreens; baby leeks and fennel; baby radishes and turnips—and the baby beets that are the Mansion regulars' all-time favorite. The chef waits to see the Tassiones' harvest, then creates a dish. A star? The beef tenderloin with duck fat fries, glazed salsify, and, for a bold counterpoint, Tassione Farms arugula. Also paired together: Paula Lambert's goat cheese with roasted beets for a toothsome twosome that's not for sissies.

Seared Gulf Red Snapper
with caramelized fennel and olive crostini

SERVES 4

To make the sauces, in a large saucepot over medium heat, heat 1 tablespoon of the extra virgin olive oil. Add the garlic and shallots and cook for 3 minutes. Add the leek, coriander seeds, fennel seeds, fennel stems, and arbol chiles and cook for 5 minutes, stirring often. Add the tomato paste, Roma tomatoes, thyme, saffron, and white wine and cover with 8 cups water. Drop the snapper bones and head and the lemon slices into the pot and cook for 45 minutes. Pass the mixture through a food mill to obtain a sauce base. Add 2 tablespoons extra virgin olive oil, salt, and pepper and set aside.

To make the fennel, in a sauté pan over high heat, heat the garlic and fennel in 2 tablespoons extra virgin olive oil. Cook for 8 minutes, or until the fennel begins to caramelize, stirring often. Add the honey and cook for 2 more minutes, then cover with the chicken stock. Reduce the heat and cook for 10 minutes, or until the liquid has evaporated. The mixture should be the consistency of marmalade. Add salt and pepper to taste and set aside.

To make the crostini, using a food processor, combine the olives, garlic, basil, extra virgin olive oil, and anchovies. Blend the mixture until smooth, season with salt and pepper, and set aside. Cut the baguette into ½-inch slices, spread the slices on a sheet pan, and toast them under an oven broiler until golden brown.

Season the fish with salt and pepper. Heat a nonstick sauté pan over high heat. Add 1 tablespoon extra virgin olive oil, place the fillet skin-side down, and cook for 5 minutes, or until the skin becomes crispy. Turn the fish and cook for 2 more minutes.

Divide the caramelized fennel among four large round plates and top with the pieces of fish. Pour the saffron sauce over the fish and serve with the black olive crostini.

SAFFRON SAUCE

3 tablespoons extra virgin olive oil
2 cloves garlic, crushed
3 shallots, peeled and sliced
1 leek, white part only, cleaned and sliced
½ tablespoon cracked coriander seeds
½ tablespoon fennel seeds
Fennel stems, chopped
2 dried arbol chiles
½ tablespoon tomato paste
2 Roma tomatoes, roughly chopped
1 teaspoon thyme
1 teaspoon saffron
½ cup dry white wine
Bones and head of a red snapper fillet
3 lemon slices
Salt and black pepper

CARAMELIZED FENNEL

1 clove garlic, crushed
2 bulbs fennel, sliced, stems removed and reserved for the sauce above
2 tablespoons extra virgin olive oil
½ tablespoon honey
2 cups chicken stock
Salt and black pepper

OLIVE CROSTINI

½ cup black olives, pitted
1 clove garlic, peeled
4 basil leaves
3 tablespoons extra virgin olive oil
2 anchovy fillets
Salt and black pepper
¼ baguette

2 (½-pound) red snapper fillets, skin on, halved (ask your fish monger to save you the bones and one fish head)
Salt and black pepper
1 tablespoon extra virgin olive oil

Game & Fowl

Roasted Pheasant

Wood Fire Grilled Squab

Grilled Spiced Bandera Quails

Flavor of Duck

Braised Rabbit Pasta

Broken Arrow Ranch Venison Loin

Grilled Cornish Hen Diablo

Whole Roasted Chicken

Chicken Thigh and Lobster

Roasted Pheasant *with dark meat strudel and Brussels sprouts*

SERVES 4

PHEASANT STRUDEL
2 whole pheasants
Salt and black pepper
1 tablespoon canola oil
1 yellow onion, sliced
2 carrots, chopped
3 cloves garlic, crushed
3 quarts chicken stock
4 sheets filo pastry
¼ cup clarified butter

APPLE CHIPS
1 cup sugar
1 apple, cored

BRUSSELS SPROUTS
1 quart Brussels sprouts, separated
½ cup diced apples (reserved from
   apple chip recipe)
4 tablespoons butter
Juice of ½ lemon
Salt and black pepper

Quarter the pheasants, or have your butcher do this for you. If you do it yourself, remove the second joint and wing tips from each bird. Remove the breasts, cutting over the ribs and along the breastplate. Cut over the wishbone and down to where the ribs connect with the wing and remove, saving the wing bone. Remove the thighs and legs. If you have your butcher do this for you, ask for the airline breasts, legs, and thighs.

Preheat the oven to 350 degrees F.

To braise the pheasant legs, season both sides of the legs with salt and black pepper. In a wide, 4-quart braising pot, heat the oil to medium and sear each side of the duck legs. Remove the seared legs and set aside. Add the onion, carrots, and crushed garlic and caramelize well. Stir and return the pheasant legs to the pot. Add enough chicken stock to cover. Bring to a simmer and cover the pot with parchment paper. Place the pot in the oven and braise for 1 hour.

Carefully remove the pheasant legs using a slotted spoon, transfer them to a sheet tray, and allow them to cool to room temperature.

Using a strainer, remove the vegetables from the pot and discard, retaining the liquid. Return the stock to the pot and cook over medium heat for 50 minutes, or until the liquid has reduced to a syrup. As it nears the syrup stage, turn the heat down to low. You may transfer the syrup to a smaller pot when the stock is reduced.

When the pheasant is cool to the touch, pull the meat and discard the bones and tendons. Place the meat in a medium mixing bowl, stir in the reduced syrup, and season with salt and black pepper.

Preheat the oven to 400 degrees F.

To make the pheasant strudel, lay out the sheets of filo pastry, and, working quickly, brush both sides with clarified butter. On the end closest to you, form the pulled pheasant meat in a finger-size line, 1 inch from the bottom of the filo pastry. Fold the bottom of the filo over the meat, roll twice, and cut off excess filo from the top. Cut into 3-inch-long rolls. Repeat this procedure using all the pastry sheets and transfer the rolls to a parchment-lined sheet tray. Brush again with the clarified butter and bake for 20 minutes, or until the filo pastry turns a golden brown.

(Continued on page 112)

(Roasted Pheasant, continued)

To make the apple chips, reduce the oven temperature to 200 degrees F.

In a 2-quart saucepot over medium heat, bring the sugar and 1 cup water to a boil and continue to boil until the sugar has dissolved, then remove from the heat.

Line a sheet tray with parchment paper. With the apple standing upright, make cuts about 1 inch away from the stem on two sides, so you are left with the center of the apple as a kind of cross-section view. With a Japanese mandoline, slice the cut sides of each side of the center of the apples. You should have a paper-thin slice of a whole apple. Dip the slices in the sugar mixture and place on the parchment-lined sheet tray. Bake in the oven for about 1 hour, or until crisp. Reserve in a covered container.

Dice the remaining ends of the apple.

In a medium sauté pan over medium heat, sauté the Brussels sprout leaves with the diced apples in the butter. Season with lemon juice, salt, and pepper.

In a large cast-iron skillet over medium heat, season the pheasant breasts on both sides with salt and black pepper and sear them in 2 tablespoons butter, skin-side down, for 4 minutes, or until the skin is crisp and golden brown. Turn the breasts over, baste them with the remaining butter in the skillet, and cook another 5 minutes. Drain the breasts on a paper towel, and slice to plate.

On each of four large serving plates, place one strudel, the Brussels sprouts, then add the sliced breasts and garnish with the apple chips.

Wood Fire Grilled Squab
with sunchoke puree

In a food processor, combine the mint, parsley, garlic, red pepper, oil, and lemon juice. Blend until the mixture is almost pureed. Season with salt and black pepper and place the split squab in a baking dish. Pour the pureed the mixture over the squab. Cover and refrigerate for 12 hours.

In a 4-quart saucepan over low heat, combine the duck fat, potatoes, garlic, thyme, and bay leaf. Cook the potatoes for 40 minutes, or until they are soft when pricked with a knife. Remove the potatoes with a slotted spoon, place them on a paper towel to dry, and set aside.

Drain the sunchokes. Place the peeled sunchokes in a 2-quart saucepot over medium heat and cover with the chicken stock. Bring to a simmer and cook for 15 minutes, or until the sunchokes are very tender. Drain and transfer to a blender. Blend, adding a little of the stock if needed to get the sunchokes moving. Add the butter while blending, 1 tablespoon at a time, until the mixture becomes a puree. Season with salt and white pepper, and set aside.

Heat a wood-burning grill to medium. Grill the squabs for 2 to 3 minutes, flip them, and grill for another 2 to 3 minutes, or until the birds are cooked through. Grill the potatoes cut-side down for 1 minute. Turn the potatoes 90 degrees and cook for another minute. Flip the potatoes and repeat the procedure on the other side. Season with salt and black pepper.

Place a large spoonful of the sunchoke puree on each plate. Cut each squab to separate the breasts from the thigh and place one of each next to the puree. Arrange the grilled potatoes on each plate and serve.

SQUAB
1 bunch mint, stemmed
1 bunch (about ½ cup) Italian parsley
4 cloves garlic
1 teaspoon crushed red pepper
1 cup canola–olive oil blend
Juice of 1 lemon
Salt and black pepper
4 squab, split, wings cut at the elbow joint, ribcage removed

DUCK FAT FINGERLING POTATOES
4 cups rendered duck fat
2 pounds fingerling potatoes, halved lengthwise
2 cloves garlic
1 sprig thyme
1 bay leaf

SUNCHOKE PUREE
2 pounds sunchokes, peeled and reserved in water
Chicken stock to cover
3 tablespoons unsalted butter
Salt and white pepper

113
GAME & FOWL

Grilled Spiced Bandera Quails
with risotto-style farro and roasted Texas peaches

SERVES 4

QUAIL MARINADE
2 tablespoons ancho chile powder
1 tablespoon ground cinnamon
1 tablespoon grated nutmeg
1 teaspoon cayenne pepper
1 tablespoon brown sugar
Juice of 2 limes
4 cloves garlic, crushed
2 tablespoons extra virgin olive oil
1 teaspoon salt
8 whole, semi-boneless quails

PEACHES
4 ripe peaches, pitted and halved
1 tablespoon ancho chile powder
Juice of 2 limes

FARRO
4 cups chicken stock
1 cup farro grains (or spelt, available
   at gourmet markets)
2 tablespoons extra virgin olive oil
3 tablespoons unsalted butter
½ carrot, peeled and cubed
1 stalk celery, peeled and cubed
½ small onion, minced
1 clove garlic, crushed
½ cup dry white wine
1 tablespoon shredded Parmesan cheese
1 tablespoon sliced scallions
Salt and black pepper

GARNISH
2 tablespoons aged balsamic vinegar
1 cup wild arugula

In a mixing bowl, combine the ancho chile powder, cinnamon, nutmeg, cayenne, brown sugar, lime juice, garlic, and oil. Mix well, and add the salt. In a baking dish, rub the quails generously with the spice mixture. Let the quails rest in the refrigerator for 1 hour.

In a mixing bowl, combine the peaches with the ancho chile powder and lime juice. Set aside.

Heat the chicken stock in a saucepot over medium heat. In a sauté pan over medium heat, roast the farro grains with 2 tablespoons of olive oil for 6 minutes, stirring often. Add 1 tablespoon of the butter and the carrot, celery, onion, and garlic. Cook for 4 minutes and add the white wine. Cook for another 3 minutes, or until the wine has evaporated.

Add one small ladle of chicken stock at a time to the sauté pan, cooking until almost all of the stock has evaporated before adding the next ladle. Repeat five or six times, or until the grains are cooked but still firm. Add another 2 tablespoons of butter, the Parmesan cheese, and the scallions. The grains should be the consistency of risotto. Season with salt and pepper and reserve warm.

Preheat the oven to 425 degrees F. Place the peaches on a baking dish and bake them for 8 minutes.

Grill the quails for 3 minutes on each side, transfer them to a baking dish, and bake them in the oven for 5 minutes.

Spoon the farro over four large plates and place the roasted peaches and the quail on top. Drizzle with balsamic vinegar and garnish with arugula to serve.

Flavor of Duck

Prepare the duck legs a day ahead of time. Rub the legs with sea salt, black pepper, thyme, and the bay leaf. Place the legs in a baking dish, cover with plastic wrap, and refrigerate for 12 hours.

The next day, heat the duck fat and garlic in a saucepot over very low heat for 10 minutes. Wash the salt from the duck legs. Dry them and cook them in the duck fat for 2 hours. Do not allow the fat to bubble. Remove the legs from the fat and pat them dry. Reserve the fat from the pan.

While the legs are still warm, remove the bones, trying to keep the legs intact. In a nonstick pan over medium heat, sear the legs, skin-side down, for 6 minutes. Place the seared legs in the oven at 400 degrees F for 6 minutes. Remove from the oven and set aside.

In a saucepot over low heat, combine the orange juice, Duck Jus, and Sriracha sauce and cook slowly for 25 minutes, or until the liquid has a glaze consistency. Set aside and keep warm.

In a saucepot with enough water to cover, boil the whole orange for 3 minutes. Drain the water, refill the pot with fresh water, and boil the orange again. Repeat this process once more, remove the orange from the liquid, and allow it to cool completely. When the orange is cool, quarter and cube the orange, keeping the peel on. Return the orange to the saucepot and add the sugar and 2 cups water. Cook the mixture over low heat for 30 minutes, or until the liquid becomes a marmalade. Set aside and keep warm.

Preheat the oven to 400 degrees F. Roast the hatch chiles on a sheet tray for 10 minutes in the oven.

(Continued on page 116)

SERVES 4

DUCK LEG CONFIT
4 duck legs, bone in
1 cup coarse sea salt
1 tablespoon black pepper
2 sprigs fresh thyme
1 bay leaf
3 cups duck fat
2 cloves garlic, crushed

ORANGE GLAZE
Juice of 4 oranges
1 cup Duck Jus (page 166)
1 teaspoon Sriracha hot sauce
   (found in Asian markets)

ORANGE MARMALADE
1 whole orange
½ cup sugar

CORN AND HATCH CHILE RELISH
2 Hatch chiles
1 tablespoon extra virgin olive oil
1 cup corn kernels
Salt and black pepper
Juice of 1 lime

ACCOMPANIMENTS
1 tablespoon extra virgin olive oil
1 cup chanterelle mushrooms,
   washed, cleaned, and dried
Salt and black pepper
2 tablespoons chopped Italian parsley
1 cup half-and-half
3 large Yukon gold potatoes, peeled
   and quartered
6 tablespoons unsalted butter, cubed

DUCK
2 (8- to 10-ounce) Peking duck breasts,
   skin on
Salt and black pepper
4 (2-ounce) raw duck foie gras slices

(Flavor of Duck, continued)

Place them in mixing bowl, cover with plastic wrap, and allow the chiles to steam for 15 minutes. Skin and seed the chiles before dicing them. In a sauté pan over high heat, combine 1 tablespoon of olive oil and cook the corn for 6 minutes. Add the chiles, and salt, pepper, and lime juice to taste. Mix well and set aside.

In another sauté pan over high heat, heat 1 tablespoon olive oil and cook the mushrooms for 6 minutes, or until their natural water evaporates. Season with salt and pepper. Garnish with the chopped parsley and set aside.

Heat up the half-and-half in a saucepot. Boil the potatoes in salted water for 25 minutes. Drain the potatoes and pass them through a food mill. Add the butter and half-and-half and mix with a whisk. Season with salt and pepper and set aside.

Season the duck breasts with salt and pepper. In a cast-iron skillet over medium heat, cook the duck breasts, skin-side down, for 8 minutes, or until the fat is rendered and the breasts are crispy. Turn the breasts over and cook for 4 minutes more. Remove the pan from the heat and let rest for 6 minutes.

Season the foie gras with salt and pepper. In a hot cast-iron skillet, sear the foie gras for 3 minutes on each side. Remove the foie gras from the pan and dry on a paper towel.

Divide the three duck preparations over four large plates: Spoon the orange glaze over the plates and cover the glaze with slices of the duck breasts. Top the breasts with the corn and Hatch chile relish. Place a generous spoon of the potatoes on the plate, topped with a piece of crispy duck confit. Finish with a slice of seared foie gras, and top with the orange marmalade and the sautéed chanterelles to serve.

Braised Rabbit Pasta
with black olives and citrus

SERVES 4

Boil the Roma tomatoes in 4 cups water in a saucepot for 10 seconds. Transfer them to an ice bath to cool. Remove the skins, then halve and seed the tomatoes before dicing them into ¼-inch cubes.

Preheat the oven to 325 degrees F. Season the rabbit with salt and pepper. In a sauté pan over medium heat, heat 3 tablespoons olive oil and sear each rabbit piece for 6 minutes, or until golden brown. Remove the rabbit from the pan and set aside.

In the same pan, sear the garlic, shallots, carrot, celery, tomatoes, and rosemary with 1 tablespoon butter for 5 minutes. Add the vinegar and white wine, and reduce the liquid by half. Add the rabbit pieces, cover with the veal stock, and cover the pan. Transfer the pan to the oven and cook for 2 hours. Transfer the pan back to the stove and remove the cooked rabbit from the pan. Cook the cooking liquid over medium heat until the liquid is reduced to a sauce consistency. Add the black olives, season with salt and pepper, and set aside.

Bring a large pot of salted water to a boil. Add the pasta and cook for 4 minutes, or until the paste is al dente. Drain, add 2 tablespoons butter, and season with salt and pepper as desired.

Place the pasta in a large, deep serving dish, then add the rabbit and sauce. Top with the lemon segments, capers, fresh oregano leaves, bread crumbs, and parsley.

BRAISED RABBIT

4 Roma tomatoes
1 whole rabbit, cut into large pieces
Salt and black pepper
3 tablespoons extra virgin olive oil
4 cloves garlic, crushed
4 shallots, minced
1 carrot, peeled and cut into ¼-inch dice
1 stalk celery, peeled and cut into ¼-inch dice
1 teaspoon dried rosemary
1 tablespoon butter
1 tablespoon balsamic vinegar
1 cup dry white wine
4 cups Veal Stock (page 165)
½ cup Kalamata olives, pitted

PASTA

2 pounds fresh tagliatelle pasta
2 tablespoons unsalted butter
Salt and black pepper

GARNISH

1 lemon, peeled and segmented
1 tablespoon capers
1 teaspoon oregano leaves
2 tablespoons bread crumbs
1 tablespoon chopped Italian parsley

 The stained glass windows in the library were brought from England by a former owner of the Mansion, Mrs. King. They bear the coat of arms of the signers of the Magna Carta at Runnymead, one of whom the owner claimed as an ancestor.

TEXANS HAVE TROUBLE QUANTIFYING THE concept of "too much"—here, everything is over the top. It was just that constant state of abundance that piqued Houston entrepreneur Mike Hughes's interest when he retired in 1983 to Ingram and started Broken Arrow Ranch. There, in the lushest part of the Texas Hill Country, wild game pretty much ran amock—Axis deer and antelope roamed far and wide; feral hogs rampaged in bulky droves, crashing through fencing and trampling down crops in an endless pursuit of food and mayhem. Native game, such as the pert whitetail deer, could barely nab a bite of cactus or grass without being shoved aside by these avid newcomers.

Hughes understood that too much of a good thing was bad. He also understood that eradicating the problem wasn't the solution. Or, at least, it wasn't a very interesting solution. Trapping and killing deer, antelope, and hogs is time-consuming, ineffective, and wasteful. So, the entrepreneurial rancher concocted the idea that a bounteous game supply could be used in a way that benefited everyone. Now Broken Arrow Ranch is operated by his son Chris, who has fine-tuned the elder Hughes's prescient notions about using what's already on the land to best advantage.

The idea was novel in the eighties, but coincided with a courageous food movement that praised and encouraged using locally grown food and game in recipes. It was strange to think of animals like the feral hog (the bane of existence for Texas farmers and ranchers) as a dining delicacy, but Hughes convinced foodies that this beast and others had found a higher purpose. Beleaguered ranchers loved the idea for obvious reasons, but so did gourmands, health enthusiasts, restaurateurs, and chefs. Even the Texas Parks and Wildlife Department loved the idea. "At the time," Chris Hughes says, "there was no reliable or good source for game meat in the world."

Also considered a nuisance, Axis deer (a favorite of chefs at the Mansion) didn't have the feral pigs' public relations problem. It's the mildest of the deer venisons and the most like fine meat minus the marbling and the fat. On the menu at the Mansion: Broken Arrow's venison loin with butternut squash gnocchi—a duet of smooth sensation that plays on both rustic and exotic reminiscence. Venison is still something of a rarity on menus because Texas deer, such as the whitetail, aren't allowed to be harvested for commercial sale (they are native, and as such belong to everyone—so, no fair selling their meat for profit). It wasn't long before restaurants began ordering game from Broken Arrow. "The Mansion was our first customer," says Hughes, "and they've been with us ever since."

Broken Arrow Ranch Venison Loin
with red cabbage compote

To make the venison sauce, combine the venison bones with the red wine, vinegar, carrot, celery, shallots, black peppercorns, juniper berries, and fresh thyme in a large mixing bowl. Marinate the bones in the refrigerator for 4 hours. After the bones have marinated, strain the mixture and reserve the liquid. Reserve the vegetables and bones separately.

In a large sauté pan over high heat, roast the bones in 3 tablespoons canola oil for 15 minutes, stirring often, until the bones turn brown. Add the reserved vegetables and cook for 10 minutes more. Add the brandy, reserved marinade liquid, and veal stock and cook over medium heat for 1 hour, or until the liquid reduces to a sauce consistency. Strain the sauce in a conical strainer back into the saucepot. Add 1 tablespoon butter, season with salt and pepper, and set aside.

To make the celeriac puree, bring the milk to a boil in a saucepan. Add the celeriac and cook slowly for 25 minutes. Drain the celeriac and blend in a food processor with 1 tablespoon of butter. Season with salt and pepper, set aside, and keep warm. (Continued on page 124)

VENISON SAUCE
4 pounds venison loin rack, bones removed and reserved (see note)
6 cups red wine
½ cup red wine vinegar
½ carrot, peeled and diced
1 stalk celery, diced
6 shallots, sliced
1 tablespoon cracked black peppercorns
1 tablespoon cracked juniper berries
2 sprigs fresh thyme
3 tablespoons canola oil
2 tablespoons brandy
4 cups Veal Stock (page 165)
1 tablespoon unsalted butter
Salt and black pepper

CELERIAC
4 cups milk
2 cups celeriac (celery root), peeled and cubed
1 tablespoon unsalted butter
Salt and black pepper

RED CABBAGE COMPOTE
1 tablespoon unsalted butter
2 cups sliced red cabbage
1 Granny Smith apple, peeled and sliced
1 tablespoon red wine vinegar
1 tablespoon sugar
Salt and black pepper

BUTTERNUT SQUASH AND COMICE PEARS
¼ butternut squash, peeled and cut into 1-inch cubes
2 tablespoons olive oil
Salt and black pepper
1 tablespoon unsalted butter
2 Comice pears, peeled, seeded, and cut into 6 pieces each

BERRY MARMALADE
2 tablespoons fresh raspberries
2 tablespoons fresh blueberries
2 tablespoons red currant jelly

2 tablespoons canola oil

This is a perfect winter dish, made with venison from the Broken Arrow Ranch in South Texas. The Mansion has been working with Broken Arrow Ranch for a long time and they deliver a great product. The ranch is very large, so while it's considered "farm raised," it's as close to wild as you can get.

(Broken Arrow Ranch Venison Loin, continued)

To make the red cabbage compote, combine 1 tablespoon butter, the red cabbage, apple, red wine vinegar, and sugar in a saucepan over medium heat. Cook over medium-low heat for 20 minutes, or until the mixture has a syrupy consistency. Season with salt and pepper and set aside.

To cook the butternut squash, preheat the oven to 375 degrees F. Lay the butternut squash cubes on a baking pan and drizzle them with olive oil. Season with salt and pepper. Bake for 15 minutes, or until the squash has caramelized. Remove the pan from the oven and set aside.

Heat 1 tablespoon butter in a nonstick frying pan and sear the pears on each side for 3 minutes, or until they are golden brown. Remove them from the pan and set aside.

To make the berry marmalade, mix the berries and jelly together in a small mixing bowl and mash them with a fork. Set aside.

Season the venison loin with salt and pepper. Sear the loin in a cast-iron skillet in 2 tablespoons of canola oil for 4 minutes on each side. Transfer the skillet to the oven and cook for 6 minutes more. Remove from the oven and let rest 5 minutes before serving.

Slice the loins. Heat the sauce and the berry marmalade in saucepots over low heat. Place the loin slices in four large, round serving plates. Arrange the cabbage, squash, and pear around the plates. Spoon the celeriac onto the plate and spread the sauce over the dish to serve.

Note: Ask your butcher to take the loin out of the rack and cut the bones for you.

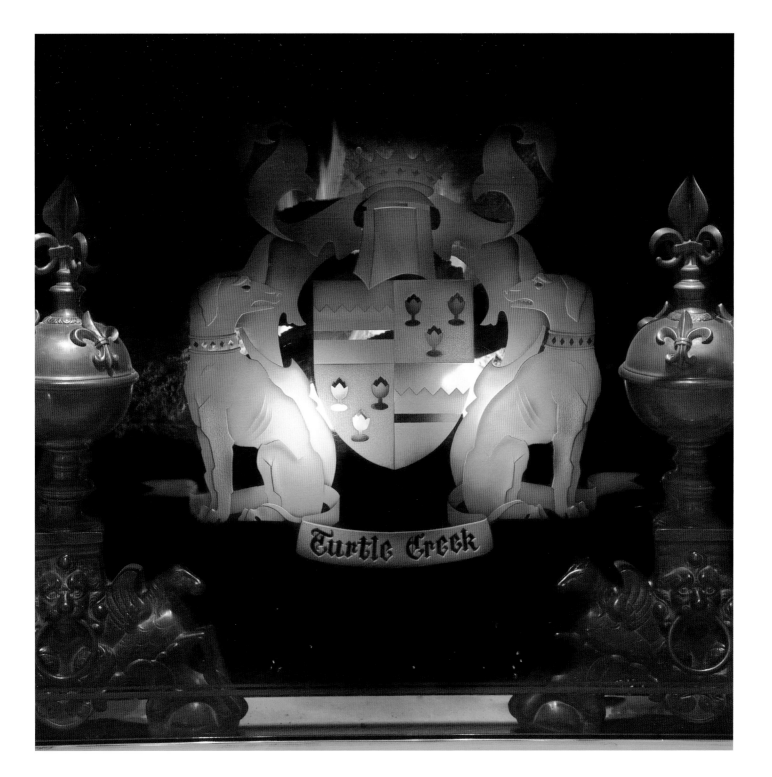

Grilled Cornish Hen Diablo
with roasted vegetables

SERVES 4

CHICKEN

2 whole Cornish hens, halved, breast
    and rib cage removed
4 cloves garlic, crushed
2 sprigs rosemary
2 sprigs thyme
1 tablespoon piment d' Espelette
    (French pepper, available in
    gourmet markets)
½ cup olive oil
Salt and black pepper
½ cup Dijon mustard

BREAD CRUMBS

1 loaf grilled Country Bread (page 46)
1 tablespoon chopped rosemary
    leaves

ROASTED VEGETABLES

2 bunches yellow, orange, and red
    baby mixed carrots, peeled
2 parsnips, peeled and cut on a bias
1 celery root, peeled and cut into
    small chunks
4 cloves garlic, crushed
2 sprigs thyme
Salt
Black pepper
2 to 3 tablespoons olive oil

DIABLO SAUCE

5 pounds chicken bones
3 tablespoons canola oil
4 shallots, sliced
1 tablespoon piment d'Espelette
¼ cup white wine
3 tablespoons sherry vinegar, plus a
    splash to finish the sauce
6 ounces canned or raw tomatoes,
    chopped
Veal Stock to cover (page 165)
2 cups Beef Jus (page 166)
2 sprigs fresh tarragon
1 small bunch chervil (similar to
    parsley, found in gourmet markets)
2 tablespoons softened unsalted
    butter

In a baking dish large enough to hold the hens, combine the crushed garlic, rosemary, thyme, Espelette, and olive oil. Mix well. Season with salt and pepper the inside and outside of each of the hen halves and place them in the marinade to coat. Cover and refrigerate for 12 hours.

To make the bread crumbs, preheat the oven to 250 degrees F. Cut the crust from the country bread and discard. Cut or tear the bread into small pieces. Place the pieces on a sheet tray and bake for 1 hour, stirring the bread pieces around the 30-minute mark. Transfer the dried bread to a food processor and pulse until crumbs are formed. In a mixing bowl, combine the bread crumbs and rosemary and set aside.

Increase the oven temperature to 350 degrees F. In a medium mixing bowl, combine the carrots, parsnips, celery root, garlic, thyme, salt, black pepper, and oil. Toss to coat. Transfer the vegetables to a roasting pan and bake for 15 to 20 minutes, or until golden brown. Remove the pan from the oven and set aside.

In a heavy-bottomed saucepan over medium-high heat, sauté the chicken bones with the oil for 30 minutes, stirring about every 7 minutes, or until caramelized. Add the shallots and the Espellette and sweat them in the pan. Deglaze the pan with the white wine and allow the mixture to reduce until almost all the liquid has evaporated. Add the sherry vinegar and reduce until it has almost evaporated. Add the tomatoes and cook for 5 minutes, or until the tomatoes start to turn brown. Pour enough veal stock into the pan so that it covers the contents of

the pan. Let this cook for 20 minutes over low heat, then add the beef jus and reduce for 15 minutes, or until the sauce has a light consistency. Remove from the heat and add the tarragon and chervil. Allow them to steep in the sauce for 15 minutes, then strain the sauce through a conical strainer. Whisk in the butter and set aside.

Preheat the grill to medium, and preheat the oven to its broiler setting. Grill the hen halves for 3 to 4 minutes on each side, or until they are just cooked through. Remove them from the grill and place on a paper towel. Brush the skin side with the Dijon mustard and coat with the rosemary bread crumbs. Place them in a baking dish and bake them under the broiler for 3 minutes, or just until they brown.

Place the roasted vegetables on four serving plates. Cut the breasts from the legs and arrange one of each on each plate. Drizzle the sauce around each dish and serve.

Whole Roasted Chicken *with tomatillo and ancho chile sauce*

SERVES 4

TOMATILLO AND ANCHO CHILE SAUCE

10 tomatillos, husks left on
2 dried ancho chiles, seeded, stemmed, and steeped in 1 cup hot chicken stock
3 cloves garlic, chopped
1 small red onion, diced
1 jalapeño, seeded, stemmed, and chopped
2 teaspoons chopped cilantro
1 teaspoon ground cumin
2 teaspoons dried Mexican oregano
1 tablespoon Champagne vinegar
2 tablespoons canola oil
Salt and black pepper

ROASTED CHICKEN

1 (4-pound) whole organic chicken
3 sprigs fresh rosemary, plus 2 for basting
3 sprigs fresh thyme, plus 2 for basting
1 lemon, sliced
Salt
Black pepper
4 tablespoons olive oil
2 teaspoons piment d'Espelette (may substitute 1 teaspoon cayenne pepper)
½ cup (1 stick) unsalted butter
1 cup chicken stock
Juice of 1 lemon
1 cup white wine

To make the tomatillo sauce, preheat the oven to 350 degrees F. Place the tomatillos on a sheet tray and roast them for 12 to 15 minutes. Remove them from the oven and set aside to cool. Keep the oven at 350 degrees F for the chicken.

When the tomatillos are cool to the touch, remove the husks and cores. In a food processor fitted with a metal blade, pulse the softened ancho chiles just until they are chopped. Add a little of the hot chicken stock if needed to process the chiles, but be careful not to puree the chiles. Add the tomatillos, garlic, onion, jalapeño, cilantro, cumin, Mexican oregano, vinegar, and oil. Pulse for a few seconds, or until well incorporated. Season the sauce with salt and black pepper to taste, transfer to a serving dish, and set aside.

Remove the wing tips and middle joints of the chicken wings. Remove the organs from the bird and discard. Stuff the bird with 3 sprigs fresh rosemary, 3 sprigs fresh thyme, and the lemon slices. Salt and pepper the inside of the bird. Using butchers' twine, tie the legs together. Line the inside of a baking dish large enough to hold the chicken comfortably with foil. Oil the bird liberally with your hands and then season well with salt, black pepper, and Espelette.

In a 2-quart saucepot over low heat, melt the butter. Add the chicken stock, lemon, white wine, and the remaining fresh herbs. Just bring the mixture to a simmer, then turn off the heat. This liquid will be used for basting the chicken during the cooking process. Roast the chicken for 50 minutes to 1 hour, basting the bird with the liquid every 7 minutes.

When the chicken is golden brown and crispy, remove it from the oven and let it rest for 10 to 15 minutes. Untie the legs and remove the herbs and lemons. Arrange the herbs and lemons on a serving platter and place the whole bird on the platter. Baste the bird once more, carve, and serve with the tomatillo and ancho chile sauce on the side.

Chicken Thigh and Lobster *"surf and turf"*

SERVES 4

Boil the lobsters in a large stockpot for 3 minutes, then transfer to an ice bath to cool. Separate the heads from the tails and remove the hard shell from the heads. Break the heads into four pieces using a large knife. Break the claws and tails and save the meat. Chop the tails into very small cubes and set aside.

In a saucepot over medium heat, combine the butter and olive oil and cook until golden brown. Add the chicken bones and roast for 4 minutes. Add the lobster heads, shallots, and garlic and cook for 6 minutes. Add the brandy to the pot, being careful as the brandy will flame up. Add the tomato, tarragon, chiles, parsley, chicken stock, and cream. Reduce the heat and cook for 25 minutes, or until the sauce becomes silky. Pass the sauce through a conical strainer and back into the pot. Season with salt and pepper to taste, and keep warm until ready to serve.

Sauté the white onion in 1 tablespoon of the olive oil for 3 minutes over medium heat. Remove from the heat and let cool. Cover the chicken thighs with plastic wrap and pound them with a heavy saucepot until they are flat.

To make the rub, combine 3 tablespoons butter, the cooked white onion, chopped lobster, egg yolks, bread crumbs, tarragon, salt, and pepper in a mixing bowl. Mix well and spread 1 tablespoon of the rub mixture over one chicken thigh, then cover with another thigh to form a sandwich. Repeat this procedure with the remaining six thighs to form 3 other sandwiches. Wrap the thighs with aluminum foil and refrigerate for 30 minutes.

Preheat the oven to 350 degrees F. Heat 2 tablespoons of olive oil in an ovenproof sauté pan over high heat and sear the chicken thighs in the aluminum on both sides for 4 minutes. Place the pan in the oven and cook for 20 minutes. Remove the aluminum packets from the pan and allow them to rest for 10 minutes.

In a sauté pan over high heat, cook the spinach and garlic in 1 tablespoon butter for 2 minutes. Season with salt and pepper and set aside. Open the aluminum packet and reserve the juices. Place the juices in a stockpot over medium heat and reheat the lobster claws in the warm juices.

Cut the thighs in half and place them on four large plates. Arrange the spinach around the thighs and place a lobster claw on the side. Add a generous portion of the sauce and serve.

Note: Ask your butcher to bone the chicken thighs for you and save the bones.

2 (1½-pound) lobsters

SAUCE
2 tablespoons unsalted butter
½ tablespoon olive oil
Bones from chicken thighs
Heads from lobsters
2 shallots, sliced
1 clove garlic, crushed
1 tablespoon brandy
1 Roma tomato, seeded and chopped
1 tablespoon fresh tarragon
2 dried arbol chiles
½ cup Italian parsley
2 cups chicken stock
1 cup heavy cream
Salt and black pepper

CHICKEN
½ white onion, minced
3 tablespoons olive oil
8 chicken thighs, deboned, skin on, bones reserved (see note)
3 tablespoons unsalted butter
2 egg yolks
1 tablespoon bread crumbs
1 tablespoon chopped tarragon
Salt and black pepper

SPINACH
2 cups baby spinach
1 clove garlic, crushed
1 tablespoon unsalted butter
Salt and black pepper

Meat

Peppered Bison Strip Loin

Herb-Stuffed Milk-Fed Veal Breast

Roasted Veal Strip Loin

Braised Pork Cheeks

Roasted Rack of Lamb

Lamb Loin

Oven-Roasted Bone-in Rib-Eye

Steak "Diane"

Beef Tenderloin

Beef Tenderloin and Spicy Short Rib Noodles

Roasted Dry-Aged Rib-Eye

Peppered Bison Strip Loin
with winter root ragout

SERVES 4

RAGOUT
4 shallots
Salt
Black pepper
Olive oil
2 salsify roots (available at gourmet
   markets), peeled, cut into 2-inch
   pieces, and reserved in lemon water
2 cloves garlic, crushed
1 pound fingerling potatoes
4 medium carrots, peeled and cut
   into 2½-inch-long pieces
2 stalks celery, cut into 2-inch-long
   pieces
2 tablespoons olive oil
4 cups chicken stock
1 sprig thyme
Juice of ½ lemon

BISON
4 (12-ounce) bison strip loins
4 tablespoons black peppercorns,
   cracked
Salt
Canola oil
1 tablespoon green peppercorns
2 tablespoons brandy
1 cup sour cream
1 cup veal demi-glace (found at
   gourmet markets)

Preheat the oven to 400 degrees F. Place the shallots in a baking dish, season with a pinch of salt and black pepper, and drizzle with olive oil. Cover the dish with foil and bake for 20 minutes. Remove from the oven, set aside, and keep warm until ready to serve.

In a mixing bowl, toss the potatoes with a pinch of salt and black pepper and 2 tablespoons olive oil. Spread the potatoes on a baking sheet and bake them in the oven for 20 minutes. Remove them from the oven and set aside.

In a sauté pan over medium heat, cook the garlic, salsify, carrots, and celery in 2 tablespoons olive oil for 6 minutes, stirring often. Add the chicken stock and thyme and continue cooking for 15 minutes more, or until all of the liquid has evaporated. Season with a pinch of salt and black pepper. Combine the potatoes and cooked vegetables in a sauté pan, season with the lemon juice, and set aside.

Crust each bison strip loin with 1 tablespoon cracked black peppercorns on one side. Season with a pinch of salt. Heat the canola oil in a large skillet and add the loins, crust-side down, and sear for 5 minutes. Turn and continue cooking for 7 minutes more. Remove the loins from the pan and allow them to rest for 5 minutes before slicing.

To the same skillet, add the green peppercorns and brandy, being careful as the brandy will flame up. Add the sour cream and demi-glace and continue cooking over medium heat for 6 minutes, or until the sauce has reduced to a silky, creamy texture. Season with salt and black pepper as desired.

To serve, place the root ragout on a large plate and arrange the sliced bison strip loin around the vegetables. Pour the green peppercorn sauce over the meat and garnish each plate with a roasted shallot.

**Any time you're cooking a piece of meat, it's best to bring it to
room temperature before cooking. Bison is a very lean meat
with a delicate flavor. You can eat it without feeling heavy.**

Herb-Stuffed Milk-Fed Veal Breast
and stewed spring vegetables

SERVES 4

To make the herb butter, combine the butter, shallot, bread crumbs, garlic, tarragon, thyme, rosemary, parsley, and lemon juice in a mixing bowl. Season the butter with salt and pepper as desired and set aside.

Preheat the oven to 325 degrees F. Pound the veal breasts with the bottom of a heavy saucepan to make them flat. Season with salt and pepper. Cover the meat with 4 tablespoons of herb butter. (Save the rest of the butter and freeze it.)

Roll up the meat and tie it firmly with butcher's twine. Let the breasts rest for 15 minutes. In a cast-iron skillet over high heat, heat 2 tablespoons olive oil and brown the meat on each side for 5 minutes. Add the garlic, fresh thyme, and 3 tablespoons water to the skillet and transfer it to the oven. Cook the veal for 2 hours, basting it often with the pan juices.

To make the veal jus sauce, boil the Roma tomatoes in a saucepot for 10 seconds. Transfer to an ice bath to cool them down. Remove the skins, then halve and seed the tomatoes before dicing them into small cubes. Warm up the veal jus in a sauté pan, and add the tomato cubes and salt and pepper to taste. Keep the sauce warm, but don't let it boil.

In a separate large sauté pan over medium heat, heat 2 tablespoons olive oil and sauté the turnips, carrots, radishes, onions, fennel, and garlic together for 5 minutes. Add 2 cups chicken stock, 1 tablespoon butter, salt, and pepper and cook for 8 minutes, or until the liquid evaporates. Set aside and keep warm until ready to serve.

Remove the veal from the oven and allow it to rest. Remove the strings and cut the veal into 1-inch slices. Transfer the meat and vegetables to a platter and serve the veal jus sauce on the side.

FRESH HERB BUTTER
- ½ cup (1 stick) unsalted butter, softened
- 1 shallot, minced
- 2 tablespoons bread crumbs
- 1 clove garlic, chopped
- 1 tablespoon chopped tarragon
- 1 tablespoon thyme leaves
- 1 tablespoon chopped rosemary
- 1 tablespoon chopped Italian parsley
- Juice of 1 lemon
- Salt and black pepper

VEAL
- 2 pounds veal breast, skin removed
- Salt and black pepper
- 2 tablespoons olive oil
- 2 cloves garlic, crushed
- 5 sprigs thyme
- 2 Roma tomatoes
- ½ cup Veal Jus (page 166)
- Salt and black pepper

VEGETABLES
- 2 tablespoons olive oil
- 1 cup baby turnips, peeled, with ½-inch stems left on
- 1 cup yellow and orange round baby carrots, peeled, with ½-inch stems
- ½ cup breakfast radishes, cleaned, with 1-inch stems
- 4 spring onions or white pearl onions, cleaned and cut into 3-inch pieces
- 1 cup baby fennel, stemmed
- 4 spring garlic (or green garlic), cleaned and cut into 3-inch pieces
- 2 cups chicken stock
- 1 tablespoon unsalted butter
- Salt and black pepper

This stuffed veal breast is an excellent cold dish as well, served with pickles and Dijon mustard and grilled country bread.

Roasted Veal Strip Loin
with carrot-cumin puree and green pea casserole

SERVES 4

CARROT-CUMIN PUREE
6 carrots, peeled and cut into 1-inch
　　pieces
2 tablespoons unsalted butter
1 tablespoon olive oil
2 teaspoons ground cumin
½ cup orange juice
4 cups chicken stock
Salt and black pepper

GREEN PEA CASSEROLE
2 cups shelled English peas
Salt
½ cup Applewood-smoked bacon,
　　cubed
½ cup white pearl onions, peeled
　　and sliced
3 tablespoons chicken stock
Black pepper
1 tablespoon unsalted butter

VEAL LOIN
½ teaspoon ground cinnamon
1 teaspoon fennel seeds
2 ½ pounds veal strip loin, cleaned
Salt and black pepper
¼ cup olive oil
2 tablespoons unsalted butter
2 cloves garlic, crushed
2 sprigs thyme
2 tablespoons honey
½ cup Veal Jus (page 166)

To make the carrot-cumin puree, sauté the carrot pieces with 1 tablespoon of the butter and 1 tablespoon olive oil in a sauté pan for 5 minutes. Add the cumin, cook for 2 minutes, and cover the carrots with orange juice and chicken stock. Cook for 25 minutes, or until the carrots are soft. Transfer the mixture to a blender and puree with 1 tablespoon butter until smooth. Season with salt and pepper as desired and set aside in a bowl.

To make the casserole, boil the peas in salted water for 3 minutes. Cool them in an ice bath and drain in a colander. In a sauté pan over medium heat, cook the bacon for 5 minutes, or until the fat is released and the bacon is crispy. Add the onions and cook for 2 minutes more. Add the peas and 3 tablespoons chicken stock, season with salt and pepper, and finish with 1 tablespoon butter. Set aside.

To prepare the veal, preheat the oven to 375 degrees F. Combine the cinnamon and fennel in a small bowl and set aside. Season the veal loin with salt and pepper. Sear the veal in the olive oil in a cast-iron skillet over high heat for 3 minutes on both sides. Remove from the heat and add 2 tablespoons of butter, 2 crushed garlic cloves, and the fresh thyme. Transfer the skillet to the oven and cook the veal for 15 minutes, basting the meat with the butter often. Remove the veal from the oven and let it rest for 8 minutes. Brush the top of the meat with honey and sprinkle with the cinnamon and fennel mixture.

Warm the veal jus in a saucepot and season with salt and pepper as needed.

To serve, place 3 slices of veal in each of four serving plates, pouring the veal jus around the plate. Display a spoonful of carrot puree on each plate and serve with the pea casserole as a side.

Braised Pork Cheeks
and creamy Homestead Gristmill grits

SERVES 4

Preheat the oven to 300 degrees F. Season the pork cheeks with salt and pepper and set them aside.

Boil the Roma tomatoes in a saucepot for 10 seconds. Transfer to an ice bath to cool them down. Remove the skins, then halve and seed the tomatoes before dicing them into small cubes. Set aside.

In a large cast-iron Dutch oven over high heat, sear the pork cheeks in the canola oil for 6 minutes, until they are golden brown. Remove the cheeks from the pot and set aside. Discard the oil. In the same pot, heat 1 tablespoon butter and cook the garlic, carrot, celery, onion, and tomato paste for 5 minutes. Add the white wine and reduce the liquid by half. Add the diced tomatoes, aji amarillo paste, and sherry vinegar and cook for 5 minutes more. Add the cheeks and the veal stock, cover the Dutch oven, and transfer it to the oven to cook for 2½ hours.

Wash the grits in cold water to extract the husk. In a large saucepan over medium heat, toast the grits with 1 tablespoons of the olive oil for 2 minutes. Add the chicken stock and cook slowly for 30 minutes, stirring often. Season with salt to taste and the ancho chile, then add the cheddar cheese, butter, and 2 tablespoons extra virgin olive oil. Keep warm until ready to serve.

In a sauté pan over high heat, heat 1 tablespoon extra virgin olive oil and cook the mushrooms for 6 minutes, or until their natural water evaporates. Season the mushrooms with salt and pepper and finish with the chopped parsley.

Remove the pork cheeks from the oven and adjust the seasoning if necessary. Divide the grits among four soup bowls, then top with the cheeks and their sauce. Spread the mushrooms around the bowl and serve.

Note: Ask your butcher to clean the pork cheeks for you.

PORK CHEEKS
2 pounds pork cheeks, cleaned
   (see note)
Salt and black pepper
3 Roma tomatoes
2 tablespoons canola oil
1 tablespoon unsalted butter
2 cloves garlic, crushed
1 carrot, peeled and diced
1 stalk celery, diced
½ medium onion, peeled and diced
1 teaspoon tomato paste
1 cup dry white wine
1 tablespoon aji amarillo paste
   (found in Asian or Latin markets)
1 tablespoon sherry vinegar
8 cups Veal Stock (page 165)

GRITS
1 cup organic white grits
3 tablespoons extra virgin olive oil
3 cups chicken stock
Salt
1 tablespoon ancho chile powder
2 tablespoons shredded sharp
   cheddar cheese
3 tablespoons unsalted butter

MUSHROOMS
1 tablespoon extra virgin olive oil
1 pound chanterelle mushrooms
   (may substitute shiitake mushrooms
   or other cultivated mushrooms),
   washed and dried
Salt and black pepper
1 tablespoon chopped Italian parsley

SHAHHAR YARDEN'S FAVORITE THING about being a miller is the way grain smells just after it's been ground. "It's a sweet, deep smell," says the miller, who is as attuned to the fresh grassy aroma as a parfumier is to the nuances of essential oils and aromatics. Yarden runs Homestead Gristmill, which is part of the Homestead Heritage Craft Village, an agricultural community near Waco. The mill is an old-fashioned operation, devoid of machinery invented during the Industrial Revolution, large-scale power mills that devastate and grind and are considered the norm today. The soft-spoken Yarden, an Israeli who emigrated to the United States, isn't an admirer: "Roller mills are an efficient way to grind flour, but they crush out all the wheat germ and the bran. Only the starch remains—and it has no nutritional value."

Diners at the Mansion recognize instantly the difference between nutritionless grain and Yarden's version. "It has a superb creamy texture," notes the chef, who tantalizes diners with ground corn's multiple personalities. As an accompaniment to braised pork cheeks, grits add calming balance; as a side to grilled shrimp and a poached egg, it's a sassy comment on a traditional Southern breakfast. Grits also appear on the Mansion menu with the roasted rack of lamb, spiced up with chimichurri sauce, and accompanying the pan-seared crab cakes and sautéed greens. Who knew that a potentially bland culinary afterthought had such wide-ranging authority?

Yarden knew, of course. The miller has a twinkle in his eye when he talks about grits. "We use high-quality organic corn that hasn't been modified in any way and is chemical-free," he enthuses. "You can tell how good the corn is by the way it smells."

And maybe that's his secret. Or, maybe it's the way the corn is stone ground in the restored mid-18th-century gristmill. "I apprenticed with an 86-year-old Scottish miller," he says, "who taught me how to use a stone mill. It's a single-pass process, where we put the grain in between the two stones mounted on a shaft. We grind it coarsely, then sift the hearts from the starch to get grits."

And that's all there is to it—or is it? Yarden admits there's more to his process, but that it eludes categorization. He can only hint that it has something to do with technique, harmony, and faith.

Roasted Rack of Lamb
with Homestead Gristmill grits fries

SERVES 4

GRITS FRIES
1 cup organic white grits
1 tablespoon olive oil
3 cups chicken stock
Salt
2 teaspoons cayenne pepper
⅓ cup shredded sharp cheddar
   cheese
Vegetable oil

CHIMICHURRI SAUCE
1 clove garlic, crushed
1 cup Italian parsley, washed and
   dried
½ cup mint, washed and dried
½ cup extra virgin olive oil
1 teaspoon cayenne pepper
1 tablespoon whole roasted almonds
1 tablespoon red wine vinegar
Salt and black pepper

LAMB
2 lamb racks (8 chops each, bones
   Frenched)
Salt and black pepper
Juice of 1 lemon
3 tablespoons extra virgin olive oil
2 cloves garlic, crushed

CHIPOTLE AIOLI
(page 164)

Wash the grits in cold water to extract the husk. In a large saucepan over medium heat, toast the grits with 1 tablespoons olive oil for 2 minutes. Add the chicken stock and cook slowly for 30 minutes, stirring often. Season with salt to taste and cayenne pepper. Add the cheddar cheese, mix well, and spread the grits into a 1-inch layer on the bottom of a baking dish.

Chill the grits in the refrigerator for 1 hour. When cold, cut large French-fry-size grits fries. Fry the grits fries in a saucepot filled with 3 inches of vegetable oil at 375 degrees F for 5 minutes, or until golden brown. Drain the fries on a paper towel and sprinkle them with salt.

To make the chimichurri sauce, combine the garlic, parsley, mint, extra virgin olive oil, cayenne pepper, almonds, and vinegar in a blender. Blend for 15 seconds to obtain a chunky sauce. Season with the salt and pepper, and refrigerate until ready to serve.

To cook the lamb, preheat the oven to 375 degrees F. Season the lamb racks with salt, pepper, lemon juice, 1 tablespoon extra virgin olive oil, and the garlic. Let marinate for 10 minutes.

In a hot cast-iron skillet, sear the racks with 2 tablespoons olive oil on both sides for 3 minutes. Transfer the skillet to the oven and cook for 12 minutes. Remove the lamb from the oven and let it rest for 5 minutes before slicing the lamb into chops.

Arrange the lamb chops on a large dish family-style with the grit fries spread around. Serve with the chimichurri sauce for the meat and the chipotle aioli for the fries on the side.

  Elizabeth Taylor was a hotel guest in 1989 and was to toss the opening coin at the Dallas Cowboys' opening game. She wanted to wear a mink coat to the game, so the hotel quickly arranged for a rack of coats to be rolled before her, so that she could pick one. The month was August.

Lamb Loin with artichoke ragu and fava beans

SERVES 4

LAMB LOIN

2 lamb racks, loins removed from
  the bone
Salt and black pepper
Juice of 1 lemon
1 teaspoon sweet paprika
½ cup extra virgin olive oil

ARTICHOKE RAGU

6 large artichokes
Juice of ½ lemon
1 cup fava beans
Salt and black pepper
4 Roma tomatoes
3 tablespoons extra virgin olive oil
4 cloves young spring garlic, washed
  and cut into 1-inch pieces
½ medium onion, minced
2 sprigs fresh thyme
4 cups chicken stock
4 basil leaves, chopped

GARNISH

1 tablespoon shaved Parmesan cheese
Extra virgin olive oil

Preheat the oven to 375 degrees F. Season the lamb loins with salt, pepper, lemon juice, sweet paprika, and 2 tablespoons extra virgin olive oil. Set aside.

While wearing gloves, remove the outer leaves of the artichokes. With a small, sharp paring knife, cut the remaining leaves away, reserving only the tender, edible artichoke hearts. Remove the center of each heart, cut into six pieces, and reserve them in water with lemon to avoid color change.

Boil the fava beans in salted water for 1 minute and transfer them to an ice bath to cool. Peel the beans and set them aside.

Boil the Roma tomatoes in a saucepot for 10 seconds. Transfer to an ice bath to cool them down. Remove the skins, then halve and seed the tomatoes before dicing them into small cubes. Set aside.

Dry the artichokes. In a sauté pan over high heat, cook the artichokes in 3 tablespoons extra virgin olive oil for 3 minutes. Add the garlic, onion, tomatoes, and thyme and cook for 3 minutes more. Add the chicken stock and cook over medium heat for 20 minutes. Season with salt and pepper and add the fava beans and chopped basil leaves. Set aside and keep warm.

On a hot open grill, grill the loins for 2 minutes on each side to create grill marks and transfer them to a baking dish. Bake the loins in the oven for 8 minutes. Remove them from the oven and allow them to rest for 6 minutes before slicing.

Cut the loins into medallions. Spread the ragu over four plates. Arrange the loin slices on top and garnish with shaved Parmesan and extra virgin olive oil.

This is a great spring dish that is made
even better by using spring garlic.

Oven-Roasted Bone-In Rib-Eye
with crispy potato pancetta cake

SERVES 4

To make the potato cake, preheat the oven to 375 degrees F. Rinse the potatoes in cold water. Drain the potatoes and dry them on paper towels. Bring a large saucepot of water to a boil. Reduce the heat and cook one third of the potatoes in the saucepot for 3 minutes, or until they begin to soften but are not fully cooked. Repeat the procedure with the remaining potatoes (if you cook them all at the same time they will stick together in the pot). Drain the potatoes and set them aside to dry.

Heat 1 tablespoon of the butter in a saucepan over medium heat. Add the garlic, onion, rosemary, and pancetta and cook for 6 minutes. Add the vinegar and cream, reduce the heat, and cook for 20 minutes to obtain a creamy consistency. Add the mustard, whisk, and season with salt and pepper.

Spread the remaining butter in the bottom of a baking dish. Place a layer of the potato slices to cover the bottom of the dish. Spread 2 tablespoons of the pancetta cream over the potatoes. Continue layering the remaining potatoes and cream in the baking dish and bake the potatoes in the oven for 45 minutes, or until the top is crispy. Remove from the oven, set aside, and keep warm.

Increase the oven temperature to 420 degrees F. Set the beef out on the counter and allow it to come to room temperature.

In a mixing bowl, combine the sea salt, black peppercorns, ancho chile, and thyme. Rub the rib-eyes with the mixture. Heat 2 tablespoons canola oil in a cast-iron skillet over medium heat and sear the beef for 3 minutes on each side. Transfer the skillet to the oven and cook for 15 minutes. Remove from the oven and allow the beef to rest for 10 minutes before slicing.

Slice the meat from the bone and serve it family-style with the potato cake. Serve with the veal jus on the side.

POTATO PANCETTA CAKE
1½ pounds Idaho potatoes, peeled
   and sliced ⅛-inch thick
2 tablespoons unsalted butter
½ clove garlic, crushed
½ cup sliced white onion
1 tablespoon chopped rosemary
¼ cup diced pancetta
1 tablespoon sherry vinegar
2 cups heavy cream
1½ teaspoons Dijon mustard
Salt and black pepper

RIB-EYE
2 (1½-pound) prime rib eyes, bone in
2 tablespoons sea salt
1 tablespoon ground black peppercorns
1 tablespoon ancho chile powder
1 teaspoon dried thyme
2 tablespoons canola oil
1 cup Veal Jus (page 166)

Steak "Diane"
with queso fresco potatoes and grilled asparagus

SERVES 8

SAUCE BASE

1 tablespoon canola oil
1 cup roughly chopped carrots
5 cloves garlic, roughly chopped
2 shallots, roughly chopped
1 cup roughly chopped onion
½ cup chopped celery
3 ancho chiles, stemmed and seeded
3 pasilla chilies, stemmed and seeded
3 New Mexico chiles, stemmed and
   seeded
1 cup red wine
½ cup brandy
2 heads garlic, halved and roasted
2 tomatoes, roasted (blackened)
2 cups veal demi-glace

SAUCE

2 shallots, minced
4 cloves garlic, minced
1 tablespoon crushed black
   peppercorns
1 tablespoon canola oil
2 tablespoons crushed green
   peppercorns
½ cup brandy
½ cup red wine
1 pasilla chile, thinly sliced
Salt
Fresh lime juice

CORN SAUCE AND POTATOES

¼ cup chopped shallots
¼ cup chopped garlic
1 cup chopped yellow onion
½ cup chopped leeks, white part only
1 yellow bell pepper, chopped
2 jalapeños, chopped
4 cups fresh corn kernels
Chicken stock to cover
Salt
Fresh lime juice
20 red potatoes, cut into 1-inch
   pieces and reserved in water
Salt and black pepper
2 tablespoons canola oil
2 cups grated jalapeño jack cheese
2 tablespoons chopped cilantro

ASPARAGUS

24 stalks asparagus, peeled, woody
   ends removed
Olive oil
Salt and black pepper

STEAKS

8 (7-ounce) prime beef tenderloin
   filets
Salt and black pepper
Canola oil
2 tablespoons unsalted butter

In an 8-quart, heavy-bottomed stockpot over medium-high heat, caramelize the carrots, garlic, shallots, and onion in the canola oil for 5 minutes. Add the celery and chiles and cook for 15 minutes more. Deglaze the pan with the red wine and reduce the liquid by half. Add the brandy and reduce by half again. Add the roasted garlic, tomatoes, and demi-glace. Cook the liquid down for 20 minutes, or until it thickens. Strain the liquid through a conical strainer, then through a fine-mesh sieve. Return the sauce base to a covered container and set aside.

To make the Diane sauce, caramelize the shallots, garlic, and peppercorns in 1 tablespoon canola oil in a 4-quart saucepan over low heat for 6 minutes. Deglaze the pan with the brandy and red wine. Reduce the liquid by half, then add 8 cups sauce base and simmer for 30 minutes, stirring constantly to prevent the sauce from sticking to the bottom of the pan. Add the pasilla chiles and season with salt and lime juice to taste.

To make the corn sauce, combine the shallots, garlic, onion, leeks, bell pepper, jalapeños, and corn in a 4-quart saucepot over high heat. Cover with the chicken stock and bring the mixture to a boil. Remove the pot from the heat, and transfer the contents to a blender. Puree the mixture for 5 minutes, then strain through a conical strainer into a container with a lid. Season with salt and lime juice and set aside.

To roast the potatoes, preheat the oven to 350 degrees F. Drain the potatoes and pat them dry. In a medium-sized mixing bowl, combine the potatoes, salt, black pepper, and oil. Toss to coat. Spread the potatoes in a sheet tray and bake in the oven for 10 to 12 minutes, or until golden brown. Remove from the oven and set aside.

To grill the asparagus, heat the grill to medium heat. Brush the asparagus with oil and season with salt and pepper to taste. Grill for 2 to 3 minutes on each side, or until the asparagus is just cooked through. Remove from the grill and place on a paper towel to drain.

Season each filet with salt and pepper. Heat a large cast-iron skillet over medium-high heat and add a little oil to the skillet. Place four of the filets into the skillet and sear each side of the filets until they have a brown crust. Add the butter to the skillet and, using a spoon, baste the filets with the butter until they are cooked to the desired temperature. Repeat with the remaining filets. Remove the beef from the pan and set them aside on a plate to rest before serving.

While the filets rest, heat the potatoes with a little butter in a large sauté pan over medium heat. Add the corn sauce just to coat the potatoes. Add the jack cheese and cilantro and toss well. Set aside.

On eight large round plates, place the filet at the 3 o'clock position. Place three asparagus stalks with one end touching the filet and the other end pointing toward the 10 o'clock position. Spoon the potatoes right where the asparagus and filet meet. Place the Diane sauce over the filet and on the bottom side of the plate and serve.

Beef Tenderloin *with duck fat fries and Tassione Farms arugula*

SERVES 4

Boil the Roma tomatoes in a saucepot for 10 seconds. Transfer to an ice bath to cool them down. Remove the skins, then halve and seed the tomatoes before dicing them into small cubes.

In a sauté pan over medium heat, cook the shallots, garlic, and honey in 2 tablespoons olive oil. Let the vegetables caramelize for 8 minutes, stirring often. Add the paprika, vinegar, tomatoes, and chiles. Reduce the heat and cook for 25 minutes, or until the mixture has a marmalade consistency. Season with salt and pepper. Discard the chiles and set aside.

In a saucepan, boil 2 cups chicken stock and the milk with the salt, thyme, and bay leaf. Add the salsify, reduce the heat, and cook for 20 minutes. Drain the liquid and reserve the salsify.

In a frying pan over high heat, sauté the salsify for 3 minutes, or until caramelized. Add the butter and 3 tablespoons chicken stock. Cook for 2 minutes. Season with salt and pepper if needed and stir in the parsley. Set aside and keep warm.

Preheat the oven to 250 degrees F. Wash the potatoes in water and dry them on paper towels. Set them aside. Warm the duck fat in a saucepot with the garlic, thyme, salt, and pepper and cook for 5 minutes over medium heat. Spread the fries in a baking dish, cover them with the hot duck fat, cover the dish with foil, and cook for 40 minutes. Remove the dish from the oven and drain the fries. In a sauté pan over high heat, fry the potatoes in 2 inches of canola oil for 5 minutes, or until golden brown. Dry them on a paper towel and season with salt.

Increase the oven temperature to 400 degrees F. Season the beef with salt and pepper.

Heat the canola oil in a skillet over medium-high heat and sear the beef for 2 minutes on each side. Add 1 tablespoon butter to the skillet and transfer to the oven to cook for 8 minutes, basting the filets frequently with the butter. Remove the beef from the oven and allow it to rest for a few minutes before serving.

Spread the salsify around four large plates and place the beef in the center. Spoon the shallot steak sauce over the beef and serve the duck fat fries on the side. Top with an arugula salad drizzled with extra virgin olive oil.

SHALLOT STEAK SAUCE

3 Roma tomatoes
6 shallots, sliced
2 cloves garlic, crushed
1 tablespoon honey
2 tablespoons olive oil
½ tablespoon sweet paprika
2 tablespoons red wine vinegar
2 dried arbol chiles
Salt and black pepper

SALSIFY

2 cups plus 3 tablespoons chicken stock
2 cups milk
Salt
1 sprig fresh thyme
1 bay leaf
1½ salsify roots (available at gourmet markets), peeled and cut into 2-inch pieces, reserved in cold water
1 tablespoon unsalted butter
Black pepper
2 tablespoons chopped Italian parsley

DUCK FAT FRIES

2 pounds large Idaho potatoes, cut into fries
4 cups duck fat
2 cloves garlic, crushed
1 sprig fresh thyme
Salt and black pepper
Canola oil

BEEF TENDERLOIN

4 (7-ounce) prime beef tenderloin filets
Salt and black pepper
2 tablespoons canola oil
1 tablespoon unsalted butter
1 cup wild arugula
Extra virgin olive oil

Beef Tenderloin and Spicy Short Rib Noodles

SERVES 4

SWEET POTATOES
2 large sweet potatoes, peeled and
    cut into ½-inch slices
2 tablespoons olive oil
1 slice bacon
1 shallot, sliced
2 cups chicken stock

BOK CHOY
1 clove garlic, crushed
2 tablespoons peanut oil
1 head bok choy, cut into large cubes
Salt and black pepper

BRAISED SHORT RIBS
2 pounds beef short ribs, uncut
Salt and black pepper
4 tablespoons canola oil
1 cup sliced shallots
1 cup sliced fennel
3 cloves garlic, crushed
1 cup white wine
1 cup rice vinegar
½ cup soy sauce
8 cups Veal Stock (page 165)
1 tablespoon coriander seeds
1 tablespoon black peppercorns
½ cup cilantro
2 stalks lemongrass, crushed

SHORT RIB NOODLES
2 cups rice noodles
2 tablespoons thinly sliced scallion
1 tablespoon thinly sliced fresh ginger
½ cup cilantro
4 tablespoons raw foie gras, cut into
    ¼-inch cubes
½ tablespoon thinly sliced Thai chile
Salt
2 tablespoons rice vinegar

BEEF TENDERLOIN
1 tablespoon canola oil
1 tablespoon unsalted butter
4 (6-ounce) beef tenderloin filets
Salt and black pepper
1 cup Veal Jus (page 166)

Preheat the oven to 350 degrees F. Cut the sweet potatoes into a square shape. In a sauté pan over high heat, sear the potatoes for 2 minutes on each side in 2 tablespoons olive oil. Transfer the potatoes to a baking dish. Cook the bacon slice and the shallot in the sauté pan for 2 minutes. Add the bacon and shallot to the potatoes and cover with the chicken stock. Cover the dish with foil and cook for 20 minutes, or until tender. Remove from the oven and set aside. Maintain the oven temperature for the short ribs.

To make the bok choy, cook the garlic in the peanut oil in a sauté pan over medium heat. Sauté the bok choy over high heat for 2 minutes, or until a nice color is obtained. Season with salt and pepper and set aside.

Season the short ribs with salt and pepper. Cook the short ribs in a cast-iron skillet over medium-high heat with 2 tablespoons of the canola oil for 5 minutes on each side. Remove the ribs from the skillet and set aside.

Add 2 tablespoons canola oil, the shallots, fennel, and garlic to the skillet and sauté over high heat for 5 minutes, or until they become translucent. Add the wine, vinegar, soy sauce, and veal stock and bring to a boil. Add the ribs, coriander, peppercorns, cilantro, and lemongrass, cover the skillet with foil, and cook in the oven for 3 hours. Remove the meat from the skillet and set aside. Pass the liquid through a strainer and reserve 2 cups liquid for the short rib noodles.

To make the short rib noodles, soften the noodles in warm water and cut them into 2-inch pieces. Heat the short ribs and noodles in the short rib braising liquid. Add the scallion, ginger, cilantro, foie gras cubes, and chile. Season with salt and rice vinegar and set aside.

In a frying pan over high heat, heat 1 tablespoon canola oil and 1 tablespoon butter. Season the tenderloin with salt and pepper. Cook the beef tenderloin for 4 minutes on each side, or until medium-rare. Let the meat rest for 5 minutes.

Heat up the sweet potatoes in a sauté pan with 1 cup of their cooking liquid, 1 tablespoon butter, and glaze for 5minutes. Warm the veal jus in a saucepot over medium heat.

Place the sweet potato and bok choy on large round plates. Place the beef tenderloin over them and spoon the jus over the tenderloin. Serve the beef short rib noodles in a small dish on the side.

Roasted Dry-Aged Rib-Eye *and braised*
short ribs with fondant potatoes

SERVES 4

Preheat the oven to 300 degrees F. Season the short ribs with salt and pepper. Heat 1 tablespoon canola oil in a sauté pan over high heat and sear the beef for 3 minutes on each side, or until both sides have a brown crust.

In a large braising pan big enough for the beef, sauté the carrots, onion, garlic, celery, and mushrooms in 2 tablespoons olive oil over high heat for 7 minutes, stirring often. Add the seared beef and cover with the red wine and vinegar. Add the bay leaf and thyme. Cover the pan with a lid and transfer it to the oven. Cook for 3 hours.

Remove the meat from the pan and let it cool. Strain the cooking liquid and discard the vegetables. When the meat is cool, cut it into 2-inch squares. Reduce the cooking liquid over medium heat until it thickens into a sauce. Add 1 tablespoon butter, salt, and pepper. Reheat the short ribs in the sauce and keep them warm until ready to serve. Increase the oven temperature to 350 degrees F.

Rinse the potatoes in a bowl of cold water. In a sauté pan over medium heat, cook the onion, garlic, and bacon in the olive oil for 5 minutes. Add the chicken stock and cook for 7 minutes. Dry the potatoes, place them in a baking dish, and cover them with the flavored chicken stock. Cover the dish with foil and cook in the oven for 35 minutes, or until tender. Remove from the oven and set aside.

In a mixing bowl, whisk the gorgonzola, sour cream, and Worcestershire sauce. Season with salt and pepper. Brush the lettuce with the cream mixture and set aside.

Increase the oven temperature to 400 degrees F. Rub the rib-eye with salt and pepper.

Heat 2 tablespoons canola oil in a skillet and sear the meat for 4 minutes on each side. Transfer the skillet to the oven and cook for 18 minutes. Remove the meat from the oven and allow it to rest for 10 minutes. Detach the meat from the bone and slice it into eight pieces.

Place the rib-eye slices on a large platter with the fondant potatoes, brushed lettuce, short ribs, and braised rib sauce. Season with a little sea salt and black pepper and serve family-style.

BRAISED SHORT RIBS
2 pounds beef short ribs, uncut
Salt and black pepper
1 tablespoon canola oil
2 carrots, peeled and sliced
1 onion, sliced
2 cloves garlic, crushed
2 stalks celery, peeled and sliced
½ cup white mushrooms, washed and halved
2 tablespoons olive oil
6 cups red wine
2 tablespoons red wine vinegar
1 bay leaf
1 teaspoon fresh thyme
1 tablespoon unsalted butter

FONDANT POTATOES
2 pounds large Idaho potatoes, trimmed to 3 x ½-inch pieces
½ onion, sliced
1 clove garlic, crushed
1 slice bacon
1 tablespoon olive oil
4 cups chicken stock

LITTLE GEM LETTUCE
½ cup mild gorgonzola cheese, at room temperature
1 tablespoon sour cream
½ teaspoon Worcestershire sauce
Salt and black pepper
2 heads little gem lettuce (or baby romaine hearts), washed and halved

RIB-EYE
1 (2-pound) dry-aged rib-eye, bone in
Salt and black pepper
2 tablespoons canola oil

Sauces & Sides

Red Mole

Tomato Chutney

Tomato Lemon Sauce

Tomato Butter

Corn and Sweet Pepper Relish

Cilantro Pesto

Tomatillo–Serrano Chile Vinaigrette

Tomatillo–Ancho Chile Sauce

Chipotle Aioli

Chimichurri Sauce

Brown Veal or Beef Stock

Veal Jus

Duck Jus

Diane Sauce

Roasted Summer Carrots

Potato Puree with Horseradish Crème

Creamy Summer Corn

Creamy Morels with Poached Organic Egg

Saffron Risotto Cake and Tomato Salsa

Sautéed Broccoli Rabe

Brazos Valley Blue Cheese Fritters

Super-Green Creamy Spinach

Grilled Asparagus

Spicy Sautéed Zucchini

Mac and Cheese

Red Mole

YIELDS 3 CUPS

1 cup peanut oil
3 dried pasilla chiles
1 dried ancho chile
2 dried guajillo chiles
2 cloves garlic, crushed
1 onion, sliced
½ teaspoon dried thyme
1 bay leaf
½ teaspoon dried marjoram
½ teaspoon ground cumin
½ tablespoon ground cinnamon
½ teaspoon ground black peppercorns
2 tablespoons sesame seeds, toasted
¼ teaspoon ground cloves
¼ cup chopped bitter dark chocolate
4 cups chicken stock
3 tablespoons bread crumbs
Salt

Place the peanut oil in a large cast-iron pot over high heat. Do not allow the oil to smoke. Fry the chiles in three batches for 20 to 30 seconds, turning them constantly. The chiles should turn bright red. Place the chiles in a mixing bowl, cover them with hot water, and soak them for 30 minutes.

Discard half of the oil in the pot and return the pot to medium heat. Add the garlic, onion, thyme, bay leaf, and marjoram and cook for 10 minutes. Add the cumin, cinnamon, black pepper, sesame seeds, and cloves and cook for 6 more minutes.

When done soaking, seed the chiles and puree them in a blender, adding a little soaking water as needed to achieve a paste consistency. Add the paste to the cast-iron pot and cook for 5 minutes more. Add the chocolate, stirring until melted, and cover the mixture with the chicken stock. Reduce the heat to low and cook for 30 minutes. Add the bread crumbs and puree the sauce in a blender until smooth. Season with a pinch of salt to taste. Keep warm until ready to serve, or store, covered, in the freezer for up to 4 weeks.

Tomato Chutney

YIELDS 2 CUPS

3 tablespoons corn syrup
1 pound green tomatoes, cubed
½ small white onion, cubed
1 teaspoon cumin seeds
Juice of 1 lemon
1 bay leaf
Salt

Cook the corn syrup in a braising pan over high heat until it is lightly caramelized. Add the tomatoes, onion, cumin seeds, lemon juice, and bay leaf. Reduce the heat to medium and cook for 20 minutes, or until it reaches a jamlike consistency. Adjust the seasoning with salt and set aside to cool to room temperature before serving.

Tomato Lemon Sauce

YIELDS 2 CUPS

Combine the tomatoes, lemons, capers, parsley, chives, extra virgin olive oil, balsamic vinegar, salt, and pepper in a mixing bowl. Cover and let the sauce marinate for 10 minutes.

1 cup teardrop tomatoes, halved
2 lemons, peeled and segmented
½ tablespoon capers
½ tablespoon chopped Italian parsley
1 tablespoon chopped chives
¼ cup extra virgin olive oil
2 tablespoons aged balsamic vinegar
Salt and black pepper

Tomato Butter

YIELDS 1 QUART

Cook the bacon in a heavy saucepan over medium heat until crispy. Add the garlic, shallots, and onions and sauté until soft. Add the tomato paste, tomatoes, and ancho chile powder and stir to combine. Add the white wine and continue cooking until the mixture is reduced by half, stirring occasionally. Add the cubed butter, a little at a time, until fully incorporated. Strain the mixture, discard the solids, and season the butter with salt and malt vinegar to taste.

1 cup chopped bacon
¼ cup chopped garlic
¼ cup chopped shallots
1 cup chopped yellow onions
1 tablespoon tomato paste
1 cup chopped red tomatoes
½ tablespoon ancho chile powder
3 cups white wine
1½ pounds (6 sticks) unsalted
  butter, cubed
Salt
Malt vinegar

Corn and Sweet Pepper Relish

YIELDS 4 CUPS

4 tablespoons (½ stick) unsalted
   butter
10 ears fresh Texas corn, kernels
   removed from the cob
1 red onion, finely diced
3 jalapeños, finely diced
5 canned piquillo peppers, diced
2 tablespoons chopped cilantro,
   plus sprigs to garnish
1 teaspoon Espelette (may substitute
   ½ teaspoon cayenne pepper)
Juice of 2 limes
1 tablespoon sherry vinegar
Salt and black pepper

In a sauté pan, melt the butter over medium heat, add the corn, and sauté for about 10 minutes, or until the kernels are tender. Transfer the corn kernels to a parchment-lined sheet tray and cool. When the corn has cooled, transfer it to a medium mixing bowl. Add the red onion, jalapeños, piquillio peppers, cilantro, espelette, lime juice, and sherry vinegar. Season with salt and pepper to taste.

Cilantro Pesto

YIELDS 2 CUPS

2 bunches cilantro, washed and
   stemmed
3 cloves garlic
½ cup pistachios
½ cup grated Parmesan cheese
½ cup olive oil
Salt
Black pepper

Combine the cilantro, garlic, pistachios, and Parmesan in a blender until the ingredients are well incorporated. Gradually add the olive oil while blending. Season with salt and black pepper to taste. Refrigerate to store.

Tomatillo–Serrano Chile Vinaigrette

YIELDS 4 CUPS

Combine the tomatillos, jicama, mango, red and yellow peppers, and serrano chiles in a medium bowl.

In a separate bowl, combine the peanut and olive oils, vinegars, and lime and lemon juices. Blend in the cilantro, garlic, and salt to taste. Pour the oil mixture over the tomatillo mixture and stir to blend. Cover and set aside at room temperature. This can be prepared several hours ahead of time and refrigerated until ready to use.

1 pound tomatillos, husks removed, diced
½ cup diced jicama
½ cup diced mango
2 tablespoons diced red bell pepper
2 tablespoons diced yellow bell pepper
2 serrano chiles, seeded and finely chopped
1 cup peanut oil
2 tablespoons extra virgin olive oil
¼ cup white wine vinegar
2 tablespoons balsamic vinegar
Juice of ½ lime
2 teaspoons fresh lemon juice
1 cup cilantro, stemmed and chopped
1 clove garlic, minced
Salt

Tomatillo–Ancho Chile Sauce

YIELDS 3 CUPS

10 tomatillos, husks left on
2 dried ancho chiles, seeded,
　stemmed, and steeped in 1 cup
　hot chicken stock
3 cloves garlic, chopped
1 small red onion, diced
1 jalapeño, seeded, stemmed, and
　chopped
2 teaspoons chopped cilantro
1 teaspoon ground cumin
2 teaspoons dried Mexican oregano
1 tablespoon Champagne vinegar
2 tablespoons canola oil
Salt and black pepper

Preheat the oven to 350 degrees F. Place the tomatillos on a sheet tray and roast them for 12 to 15 minutes. Remove them from the oven and set aside to cool.

When the tomatillos are cool to the touch, remove the husks and cores. In a food processor fitted with a metal blade, pulse the softened ancho chiles just until they are chopped. Add a little of the hot chicken broth if needed, but be careful not to puree the chiles. Add the tomatillos, garlic, onion, jalapeño, cilantro, cumin, Mexican oregano, vinegar, and oil. Pulse for a few seconds, or until well incorporated. Season the sauce with salt and black pepper to taste, and transfer to a serving dish, or refrigerate until ready to use.

Chipotle Aioli

YIELDS 4 CUPS

1 (7.5-ounce) can chipotle peppers
5 egg yolks plus 1 whole egg
3 cloves garlic
Juice of 2 limes
3 cups canola oil
Pinch salt

In a food processor fitted with a metal blade, puree the canned chipotles. Add the egg yolks and eggs, garlic, and lime juice. While the food processor is running, slowly add the oil and season with salt.

Chimichurri Sauce

YIELDS 3 CUPS

Combine the garlic, parsley, mint, extra virgin olive oil, cayenne pepper, almonds, and vinegar in a blender. Blend for 15 seconds to obtain a chunky sauce. Season with salt and pepper and refrigerate until ready to serve.

1 clove garlic, crushed
1 cup Italian parsley, washed and dried
½ cup mint, washed and dried
½ cup extra virgin olive oil
1 teaspoon cayenne pepper
1 tablespoon whole roasted almonds
1 tablespoon red wine vinegar
Salt and black pepper

Brown Veal or Beef Stock

YIELDS 4 QUARTS

Preheat the oven to 425 degrees F.

Spread the bones in a roasting pan and roast them for 30 minutes, turning once. Remove the pan from the oven and paint a thin layer of tomato paste over the bones. Place the celery, carrot, and onions on top of the bones, return the pan to the oven, and roast for an additional 15 to 20 minutes, or until the vegetables begin to caramelize.

Transfer the bones and vegetables to a stockpot. Deglaze the roasting pan with wine or water and pour this liquid into the stockpot. Add the peppercorns, bay leaves, thyme, and enough cold water to cover the bones.

Over medium heat, slowly bring the bones to a gentle simmer. Do not let the stock boil. Adjust the temperature to maintain a gentle bubbling simmer. Let the stock simmer gently for at least 4 or up to 12 hours. Every half hour, skim off any foam that rises to the top. Add a little more water and lower the heat if the stock reduces too quickly.

When the stock is done, remove the bones and discard. Strain the liquid through a very-fine-mesh strainer or a colander lined with three or four layers of cheesecloth. Chill quickly, then refrigerate. Before using, skim off the solidified fat and discard.

7 pounds veal or beef bones, cut into
   2 or 3-inch pieces
1 (8-ounce) can tomato paste
1 cup chopped celery
1 cup chopped carrot
2 cups chopped onions
1 cup red wine or water, for
   deglazing
Small handful black peppercorns
4 bay leaves
3 sprigs thyme

Veal Jus

2 pounds fresh veal breast, roughly
    cubed (or the scraps and bones
    from veal rack)
3 tablespoons canola oil
Unsalted butter, as needed
2 cloves garlic, crushed
1 cup sliced scallions
1 carrot, cut into large cubes
1 Roma tomato, halved
1 cup dry white wine
8 cups Veal Stock (page 165)
2 sprigs fresh thyme

In a large saucepot over high heat, sear the veal breast or scraps and bones in the canola oil for 10 minutes on each side, or until caramelized. Add butter, if necessary, to help the caramelization process. Add the garlic, scallions, carrot, and tomato and cook for 8 minutes more. Add the white wine and continue to cook until the liquid has reduced by half. Add the veal stock and thyme and cook over medium-low heat for 1 hour. Pass the liquid through a conical strainer and store in a covered container in the refrigerator for up to 1 week.

Duck Jus

YIELDS 2 CUPS

2 pounds duck parts (necks or body),
    cut into pieces
3 tablespoons canola oil
2 cloves garlic, crushed
1 cup sliced shallots
1 carrot, cubed
1 lemon, sliced
Unsalted butter, as needed
½ cup balsamic vinegar
2 sprigs fresh thyme
8 cups Veal Stock (page 165)

In a large saucepot over high heat, sear the duck bones in the canola oil for 10 minutes, or until caramelized. Add the garlic, shallots, carrot, and lemon and cook for 8 minutes. Add a little butter, if necessary, to help with the caramelization process. Add the vinegar and reduce the liquid by half. Add the veal stock and thyme, and cook over medium-low heat for 1 hour. Pass the jus through a conical strainer and store in a covered container in the refrigerator for up to 1 week.

Diane Sauce

YIELDS 2 QUARTS

In an 8-quart, heavy-bottomed stockpot over medium-high heat, caramelize the carrots, garlic, shallots, and onions in the oil for 6 mintues. Add the celery and chiles and cook for 15 minutes more. Deglaze the pan with the red wine and reduce the liquid by half. Add the brandy and reduce by half again. Add the roasted garlic, tomatoes, and demi-glace. Cook the liquid down for 20 minutes, or until it thickens. Strain the liquid through a conical strainer, then through a fine-mesh sieve. Return the liquid to a covered container and set aside.

Caramelize the shallots, garlic, and peppercorns in the oil in a 4-quart saucepan over low heat for 5 minutes. Deglaze the pan with the brandy and red wine. Reduce the liquid by half, then add the base and simmer for 30 minutes, stirring constantly to prevent the sauce from sticking to the bottom of the pan. Add the pasilla chiles and season with salt and lime juice to taste.

BASE
1 cup roughly chopped carrots
5 cloves garlic, roughly chopped
2 shallots, roughly chopped
1 cup roughly chopped onions
3 tablespoons canola oil
½ cup chopped celery
3 ancho chiles, stemmed and seeded
3 pasilla chiles, stemmed and seeded
3 New Mexico chiles, stemmed and seeded
1 cup red wine
½ cup brandy
2 bulbs garlic, halved and roasted
2 tomatoes, roasted (blackened)
2 cups veal demi-glace

SAUCE
2 shallots, minced
4 cloves garlic, minced
1 tablespoon crushed black peppercorns
2 tablespoons crushed green peppercorns
1 tablespoons canola oil
½ cup brandy
½ cup red wine
1 pasilla chile, finely sliced
Salt
Fresh lime juice

Roasted Summer Carrots
with cumin and lemon

SERVES 4

Preheat the oven to 375 degrees F. Peel the carrots, leaving a 1-inch stem. Cut the carrots in half lengthwise.

Juice 1 lemon in a mixing bowl. Add the honey, cumin, garlic, and olive oil, and season with salt and pepper to taste. Place the carrots in a roasting pan. Drizzle the lemon and honey mixture evenly over the carrots. Cover the pan with aluminum foil and cook for 20 minutes, or until the carrots start to caramelize.

Garnish with the chopped Italian parsley before serving.

2 pounds young carrots, with stems
1 lemon
1 tablespoon honey
½ tablespoon ground cumin
2 cloves garlic, crushed
2 tablespoons extra virgin olive oil
Salt and black pepper
½ bunch Italian parsley, chopped, for garnish

Potato Puree with horseradish crème

SERVES 4

Preheat the oven to 375 degrees F. Cover a sheet tray with the sea salt and place the potatoes over the top. Place the sheet in the oven and roast the potatoes for 2 hours, or until they are tender. Remove the tray from the oven. Peel the potatoes while they are still warm (you may need to wear 2 layers of disposable gloves to protect your hands from the heat). Pass the potato flesh through a ricer, or use a potato masher, then combine the potatoes, butter, and warm milk in a saucepan over medium-low heat. Cook for 3 minutes, stirring constantly. Season the potatoes with salt and white pepper to taste.

Combine the crème fraîche and horseradish in a mixing bowl and season with salt and white pepper to taste.

Transfer the potatoes to a serving dish and garnish with a dollop of the horseradish crème and chives to serve.

Sea salt
4 Idaho potatoes
4 tablespoons (1/2 stick) unsalted butter
½ cup whole milk, warm
Salt
White pepper

HORSERADISH CRÈME
2 cups crème fraîche
¼ cup grated fresh horseradish
Salt and white pepper
2 tablespoons chopped chives, for garnish

Creamy Summer Corn *with crispy bacon*

SERVES 4

CORN VELOUTÉ
4 cups fresh corn kernels
6 cups vegetable stock
Salt and black pepper

SOUP
2 sprigs fresh thyme
2 sprigs fresh parsley
10 peppercorns
10 ears corn, kernels cut off, cobs
  reserved
4 quarts chicken stock
1 cup heavy cream
2 sprigs parsley, finely chopped
2 sprigs thyme, finely chopped
½ cup (1 stick) unsalted butter,
  cut into ½-inch cubes
¼ cup chopped scallions
Salt
Black pepper
½ pound bacon, diced and cooked
  until crispy, for garnish

To make the velouté, cook the corn in the vegetable stock in a large stockpot over low heat for 2 hours. Puree the mixture in a blender and season as desired with salt and pepper. Strain the liquid through a fine sieve, discard the solids, and set aside in a bowl.

Tie the thyme and parsley sprigs and peppercorns together in a cheesecloth using butcher string. Combine the corn kernels, cobs, bundle of herbs, and chicken stock in a wide saucepot, cover with parchment paper, and cook over medium heat for 20 to 30 minutes, or until the corn is tender. Remove the corn from the heat and allow to cool. When the corn is cool enough to handle, scrape the cobs with the back of a knife to release their juices into the pot and discard the cobs. Strain the corn mixture to remove any excess liquid and reserve the corn kernels and 1 cup of the corn stock.

In a large saucepot over medium-high heat, combine the corn stock and heavy cream and cook for 20 to 30 minutes, or until the liquid is reduced by half. Reduce the heat to medium and add the cooked corn, ½ cup corn velouté, chopped parsley, and chopped thyme. Slowly stir in the cubed butter a little at a time and continue cooking about 7 minutes, or until the corn is creamy. Fold in the scallions and season with salt and black pepper to taste. Transfer to a serving dish and garnish with crispy bacon.

Creamy Morels *with poached organic egg*

SERVES 4

To make the mushroom stock, sweat the onion over medium heat in a dry, wide, heavy-bottomed pan for about 3 minutes, or until it becomes soft and translucent—do not let the onion brown. Add the mushrooms, thyme, and bay leaves and continue cooking for 5 minutes, or until all of the liquid has evaporated. Add 3½ quarts cold water, reduce the heat to low, and steep for 45 minutes. Do not simmer. Strain and discard the solids and allow the broth to cool.

In a sauté pan over medium heat, cook the shallots in the butter for 5 minutes, or until they become soft and translucent. Add the morels and cook for 5 more minutes. Add ½ cup of the mushroom stock and continue cooking until almost all of the liquid has evaporated; there should be only about 3 tablespoons liquid left in the pan. Add the heavy cream and continue cooking for 5 minutes, or until the morels are creamy. Season with a pinch of salt and black pepper to taste.

Bring 3 quarts of water and vinegar to a simmer in a separate saucepan. Poach the eggs: 2½ minutes for a soft poach, 4 minutes for a medium poach, and 8 minutes for a hard poach.

To serve, divide the morels among four bowls and top each serving with chives and a poached egg. Drizzle with extra virgin olive oil and sprinkle each egg with a pinch of fleur de sel.

MUSHROOM STOCK
1 yellow onion, thinly sliced
2 pounds button mushrooms, cleaned and sliced
1 sprig fresh thyme
3 bay leaves

MORELS
2 shallots, minced
2 tablespoons unsalted butter
1 pound morels, cleaned
½ cup heavy cream
Salt
Black pepper

1 teaspoon white vinegar
4 organic eggs
2 tablespoons chopped chives
1 tablespoon extra virgin olive oil
1 teaspoon fleur de sel

Saffron Risotto Cake and Tomato Salsa

SERVES 4

RISOTTO

8 cups chicken stock
1 tablespoon saffron threads
2 tablespoons minced shallot
1½ tablespoons minced garlic
4 tablespoons (½ stick) unsalted
  butter
2 cups carnaroli rice, or good risotto
½ cup white wine
2 cups grated Parmesan cheese
¼ cup thinly sliced scallions, white
  part only
Salt and black pepper
Juice of 1 lemon
Vegetable oil

TOMATO SALSA

6 Roma tomatoes, roughly chopped
5 cloves garlic, roasted
3 large shallots, chopped
1 cup fresh basil leaves
¼ cup balsamic vinegar
1 tablespoon honey
Juice of 1 lime
½ cup olive oil
Salt and black pepper

Bring ½ cup of the chicken stock to a boil in a small saucepan, remove the pan from the heat, add the saffron, and allow it to steep for 10 minutes.

In a separate 4-quart, heavy-bottomed saucepan over medium-high heat, sauté the minced shallot and garlic in 2 tablespoons of the butter until tender. Add the rice and continue to stir for about 2 minutes. Add the white wine and stir constantly until almost all the liquid has evaporated. Add enough chicken stock to barely cover the rice and cook, stirring occasionally. Once the chicken stock is almost completely absorbed, again add enough chicken stock to barely cover the rice. Repeat this procedure several times, covering the rice with the stock until the rice is cooked and all of the stock is absorbed. The rice will still have a little bite to it.

Reduce the heat by half and stir in the grated Parmesan, scallions, and the bloomed saffron. Continue stirring until the risotto is creamy. Stir in the remaining butter and season with salt, black pepper, and lemon juice to taste. Line a baking sheet with parchment and coat the parchment with nonstick spray. Spread the risotto over the parchment and use a spatula to smooth it out evenly into a 1-inch-thick layer. Refrigerate the pan of risotto for 1 hour.

While the risotto is chilling, make the salsa. Combine the tomatoes, garlic, shallots, basil, balsamic vinegar, honey, and lime juice in a food processor and pulse until all the ingredients are well incorporated. Pour the mixture into a bowl and gradually whisk in the olive oil until fully incorporated. Season the salsa with salt and pepper and set aside.

Preheat the oven to 375 degrees F. Once the risotto is cool, use a 3-inch round cutter to cut four uniform circles of risotto. In a sauté pan, heat ½ inch of vegetable oil over medium heat until the oil is almost smoking. Fry the risotto cakes for 2 minutes on each side. Place the fried cakes in the oven for 7 minutes, then allow the baked cakes to drain on a paper towel. Serve the risotto cakes over the tomato salsa.

Sautéed Broccoli Rabe
with red chile and fried garlic

SERVES 4

To make the concassé tomatoes, bring 4 quarts salted water to a boil. In a large mixing bowl, prepare 4 quarts ice water. Cut a small X on the bottom of each tomato with a sharp knife. Add the tomatoes to the boiling water for 40 seconds, then cool them in the prepared ice bath. When completely cooled, peel (pulling the skin from the X) and chop the tomatoes, discarding the seeds.

Combine the tomatoes, white wine, and vinegar in a saucepan over low heat and cook, stirring constantly, for 1 hour or until all of the liquid has evaporated. The mixture should look like a paste. Remove from the heat and cool completely. Once cool, add the tarragon, chives, and olive oil and whisk to combine. Season with a pinch of salt and pepper and set aside in a bowl.

In a sauté pan over medium heat, sauté the garlic in 1 tablespoon butter. Add the the broccoli rabe, 1 tablespoon concassé tomatoes, and crushed red pepper. Cook for 2 to 3 minutes. Add the chicken stock and continue cooking for 2 minutes. Season with a pinch of salt and black pepper to taste and serve.

CONCASSÉ TOMATOES WITH OLIVE OIL
Salt
10 Roma tomatoes
1 cup dry white wine
½ cup Champagne vinegar
1 tablespoon chopped tarragon
1 tablespoon chopped chives
2 tablespoons extra virgin olive oil
Black pepper

3 cloves garlic, thinly sliced
1 tablespoon unsalted butter
3 bunches broccoli rabe, cleaned,
    stems trimmed to 2 inches
1 teaspoon crushed red pepper
¼ cup chicken stock
Salt and black pepper

173

Brazos Valley Blue Cheese Fritters

SERVES 4

To make the fritter batter, combine the blue cheese, butter, and Worcestershire sauce in a food processor and process until smooth. Season with salt and black pepper to taste and transfer the mixture to a pastry bag. Pipe the mixture onto a parchment-lined baking sheet to form 1-inch balls. Cover the baking sheet and freeze for 3 hours.

In a medium bowl, season the flour with a pinch of salt and black pepper. Put the egs in a separate bowl, and use a third bowl for the bread crumbs. Toss the frozen balls in the flour, then dip them in the beaten egg, followed by the bread crumbs to coat completely. Place the balls in a container, cover, and return them to the freezer. These can be prepared ahead and will keep in the freezer in a covered container for 1 month.

When you are ready to fry the fritters, heat the grapeseed oil to 360 degrees F and fry the frozen blue cheese balls, six at a time, for 4 to 6 minutes, or until golden brown. Drain on a paper towel.

4 ounces Brazos Valley blue cheese
3 tablespoons unsalted butter, softened
½ teaspoon Worcestershire sauce
Salt and black pepper
1 cup flour
4 eggs, beaten
2 cups panko (Japanese bread crumbs)
2 cups grapeseed oil

In 1936 President Franklin D. Roosevelt visited Dallas to unveil a statue of Robert E. Lee at the newly named Lee Park. He stayed at the Mansion, then the private residence of the Burfords, in a large room on the second floor. It's now known as the FDR Suite, and used as a private dining room.

Super-Green Creamy Spinach

MORNAY SAUCE
2 cups heavy cream
2 cups whole milk
½ cup grated white cheddar cheese
½ cup grated Parmesan cheese
½ cup grated pecorino cheese
2 tablespoons unsalted butter
2 tablespoons all-purpose flour
Salt and white pepper

SPINACH PUREE
1 tablespoon baking soda
2 bunches spinach, cleaned and
   stemmed

SPINACH
Salt
6 bunches spinach, cleaned and
   stemmed
¼ cup chicken stock
Cracked black pepper

SHALLOT CRUST
4 cups peanut oil
5 medium shallots, thinly sliced
2 cups flour, seasoned with salt and
   black pepper
2 cups panko (Japanese bread crumbs)

To make the mornay sauce, combine the heavy cream and milk in a saucepan over medium heat and bring the mixture to a simmer. Add the white cheddar, Parmesan, and pecorino cheeses, stirring constantly with a wire whisk until the cheeses are melted. In a separate saucepan, melt the butter over medium heat, add the flour, and cook for 7 minutes, stirring constantly. Add the butter and flour to the cheese mixture, stirring constantly, until fully incorporated. Reduce the heat by half and continue cooking for 20 minutes, stirring occasionally. Pour the sauce into a bowl, season with salt and white pepper to taste, and set aside.

Make the spinach puree by combining 6 cups cold water with the baking soda and the cleaned spinach in a 2-quart saucepan over high heat. Bring the spinach to a boil, stirring frequently. Cook for 1 minute. Drain the spinach in a colander, squeeze out the extra liquid, and transfer it to a blender. With as little water as possible in the blender, puree the spinach mixture on high until it is smooth. Strain the mixture through a fine sieve. Set aside in a bowl.

Bring 4 to 5 quarts heavily salted water to a boil. Add the clean fresh spinach and boil for 3 minutes. Remove the spinach from the hot water and plunge it into an ice water bath to stop the cooking. Drain the spinach and squeeze out the excess water.

In a saucepan over medium heat, combine 1 cup mornay sauce, the chicken stock, and cooked spinach and cook for 5 minutes. Add 4 tablespoons of the spinach puree and salt and pepper to taste.

To make the shallot crust, heat the oil to 360 degrees F in a Dutch oven. Dredge the shallot rings in seasoned flour, shake off the excess, and fry the rings in small batches for about 3 minutes, turning, until they are golden brown. Drain the fried shallots on a paper towel and allow them to cool. Once cooled, combine the fried shallots and bread crumbs in a food processor and pulse 6 to 7 times, or until well combined. Transfer the spinach to an ovenproof serving dish, coat the top with the shallot crust, and broil in the oven for about 2 minutes, or until golden brown. Serve family style.

Note: This recipe can also be prepared in individual baking dishes.

Grilled Asparagus *with olive oil and mint*

To make the oil, bring a saucepot of water to a boil and blanch the mint leaves in the boiling water for 2 minutes. Remove the leaves from the hot water and shock them in an ice bath. When the leaves are cool, squeeze out any excess water. Combine the mint, parsley, and canola oil in a blender and puree until smooth. Return the oil to a saucepan over medium heat and cook for 5 minutes, or until the mixture turns a vibrant green color. Pour the mixture into a conical strainer fitted with a coffee filter and allow the oil to drain into a bowl for 1 hour. Transfer the oil to a squeeze bottle and chill in an ice bath until it has completely cooled.

Preheat the grill to medium heat. Brush the asparagus with olive oil and season with salt and pepper. Grill the asparagus for 2 to 3 minutes on each side, or until just cooked through. Transfer the asparagus to a serving platter. Drizzle the asparagus with olive oil and mint oil. Sprinkle with fresh mint and serve.

MINT OIL
¼ pound fresh mint, cleaned and
  stemmed
1 bunch (about ½ cup) fresh parsley
  leaves
1 cup canola oil

ASPARAGUS
1½ pounds asparagus, trimmed
Extra virgin olive oil, for brushing
  asparagus, plus 4 tablespoons to
  drizzle
Salt and black pepper
2 tablespoons mint cut into thin
  strips

Spicy Sautéed Zucchini

Cook the shallots in 2 tablespoons of the olive oil in a sauté pan over medium heat until they are soft and translucent. Add the zucchini, tagashari, garlic, and basil and cook until the zucchini becomes tender. Transfer the zucchini to a serving dish. Drizzle with the remaining extra virgin olive oil, season with salt and black pepper to taste, and serve.

2 shallots, minced
5 tablespoons extra virgin olive oil
3 zucchini, cut into medium dice
1 teaspoon tagashari (Japanese pepper
  spice, found in Asian markets)
3 cloves garlic, crushed
1 sprig basil, stemmed
Salt and black pepper

Mac and Cheese with ham

SERVES 4

Salt
16 ounces elbow macaroni

MORNAY SAUCE
2 cups milk
2 cups heavy cream
1 onion, peeled and halved
3 cloves
2 tablespoons unsalted butter
2 tablespoons flour
¾ cup grated shredded Gruyère cheese
Salt and black pepper
1 cup crème fraîche

MAC AND CHEESE
8 ounces smoked black forest ham,
  diced
1 cup diced Gruyère cheese
Salt and black pepper
2 cups bread crumbs

Bring a pot of salted water to a boil. Add the elbow macaroni and cook for 8 minutes. Drain and rinse.

To make the mornay sauce, combine the milk, cream, onion, and cloves in a saucepot over medium heat and bring to a boil. In a separate saucepot over medium heat, melt the butter and add the flour. Cook, stirring constantly, for 3 minutes. Whisk the butter-flour mixture into the hot milk mixture, reduce the heat to low, and continue cooking for 15 minutes, stirring occasionally. Remove from the heat, add the cheese, and season with salt and black pepper. Pass through a conical strainer and discard solids. Stir in the crème fraîche.

Preheat the broiler.

Combine the pasta, 2 cups mornay sauce, the ham, cheese, and salt and black pepper in a pot and cook over medium heat until heated through. Pour into a gratin dish and top with bread crumbs. Broil until golden brown, about 2 minutes.

Hotel guest singer Patti LaBelle protested that there was no soul food on the room service menu, so the kitchen quickly improvised a soul food meal and delivered it to her. She was so delighted she ordered the same meal the next night from room service.

Brunch

Mansion Eggs Benedict

Cinnamon Brioche French Toast

Grilled Shrimp with Homestead Gristmill Grits

Mansion on Turtle Creek Granola

Huevos Rancheros

Zucchini and Ricotta Cannelloni

Fire-Roasted Chile Rellenos

Foie Gras Doughnuts

Mansion Eggs Benedict

SERVES 4

4 pounds creamer fingerling potatoes,
   halved lengthwise
2 tablespoons canola oil
Salt
Black pepper
3 shallots, sliced
1 tablespoon unsalted butter
2 tablespoons chopped parsley
1 tablespoon chopped fresh thyme
2 (7-ounce) beef tenderloin filets,
   sliced into 8 (¼-inch-thick) rounds
12 asparagus spears, peeled
1 teaspoon distilled vinegar
8 eggs
4 English muffins, halved and toasted
2 tablespoons chopped chives, for
   garnish

HOLLANDAISE SAUCE
2 egg yolks
2 teaspoons fresh lemon juice
Dash Tabasco sauce
Salt
Cracked black pepper
½ cup (1 stick) unsalted butter,
   melted

Preheat the oven to 350 degrees F. Toss the potatoes with 1 tablespoon canola oil, and salt and black pepper to taste and place them in a single layer on a cookie sheet. Bake for 12 minutes. Remove from the oven and set aside.

In a sauté pan over medium heat, cook the shallots in 1 tablespoon canola oil and 1 tablespoon butter until caramelized. Add the potatoes, parsley, thyme, and salt and pepper to taste and toss. Cook for a few minutes more until the potatoes are golden brown.

Heat a griddle over medium-high heat and season the filets with salt and pepper on both sides. Cook on the griddle for 2 to 3 minutes on each side for medium-rare steaks. Remove from the heat and allow the steaks to rest.

To make the Hollandaise sauce, whisk the egg yolks with the lemon juice, hot sauce, and 2 teaspoons water in a stainless-steel bowl set over a pot of simmering water until the mixture is pale yellow in color. Be careful not to let the bowl touch the water. Season with salt and pepper as desired. Remove the bowl from the pot and add the butter 1 teaspoon at a time, whisking vigorously, until all is incorporated. Cover the sauce and keep it in a warm place until you are ready to serve.

Boil the asparagus in a pot of generously salted water for 5 minutes. Remove the asparagus from the hot water and place it directly in an ice bath to maintain its green color. Drain on a paper towel and set aside.

Just before serving, bring 12 cups water and 1 teaspoon distilled vinegar to a simmer in a saucepan. Poach the eggs, four at a time: 2½ minutes for a soft poach, 4 minutes for medium, and 8 minutes for a hard poach.

To assemble the eggs benedict, spoon a portion of the potatoes onto the center of a serving plate and top with 3 asparagus spears. Top with 2 English muffin halves and a filet round. Top each filet with a poached egg and sauce each egg with 2 tablespoons Hollandaise. Garnish with chopped chives and serve.

Cinnamon Brioche French Toast

SERVES 8

CINNAMON BRIOCHE LOAF
(Yields two 5 x 8-inch loaves)
2 envelopes active dry yeast
¼ cup plus 3 tablespoons sugar
1 teaspoon salt
8 extra large eggs, at room
   temperature
5 to 5 ½ cups all-purpose flour
1 ½ cups (3 sticks) unsalted butter,
   softened
3 tablespoons ground cinnamon

FRENCH TOAST
2 extra large eggs, lightly beaten
⅔ cup milk
¼ teaspoon salt
4 tablespoons unsalted butter
8 (1-inch thick) slices Cinnamon
   Brioche Loaf
Pure maple syrup

To begin the brioche loaf, combine the yeast and ¼ cup sugar with ½ cup warm water, stirring with a fork to dissolve. Let the yeast sit until the mixture becomes foamy.

Place the salt and eggs in the large bowl of a mixer fitted with a dough hook. Beat the eggs lightly and add the yeast mixture, then gradually add the flour to make a soft dough, mixing constantly. With the mixer running, add the butter, 2 tablespoons at a time, until it is fully incorporated. The dough will be soft. Using the dough hook, knead for about 5 minutes (the dough will be too sticky to knead by hand).

Place the dough in a large, greased mixing bowl. Cover the bowl loosely with plastic wrap and a cloth towel. Set in a warm place, free from drafts, for about 1½ hours, or until the dough has risen and doubled in size. When it has doubled, punch down the dough in the bowl, cover tightly with plastic wrap, and refrigerate for 8 hours or overnight.

Grease two 5 x 8-inch loaf pans. Divide the cold dough into two pieces. On a lightly floured board, roll each piece into an 8-inch square. In a small bowl, combine 3 tablespoons sugar and the cinnamon. Sprinkle equal amounts of the cinnamon-sugar over each piece of dough and roll the dough up as you would a jelly roll. Place the rolls in the prepared pans. Cover the pans with a towel and set in a warm place, free from drafts, to rise for 1 hour, or until the brioche mounds about 1 inch above the edge of the pan.

Preheat the oven to 400 degrees F. When the brioche has risen, bake in the preheated oven for 30 minutes, or until the loaf sounds hollow when tapped. Remove the loaves from the oven and immediately turn out onto a rack. Cool before cutting.

To make the French toast, beat the eggs with the milk and salt to blend. Melt about 2 tablespoons butter in a large, heavy skillet. Dip one slice of bread in the egg mixture, coating both sides well. Fry the bread for about 1 minute on each side, or until light brown. Repeat until all the slices are brown, adding more butter as needed. Keep the toasts warm until ready to serve. Cut the slices in half and serve warm with pure maple syrup.

Grilled Shrimp
with Homestead Gristmill grits and poached egg

SERVES 4

To make the concassé tomatoes, bring 4 quarts salted water to a boil. Put 4 quarts ice water in a large mixing bowl. Cut a small, shallow X on the bottom of each tomato with a sharp knife. Add the tomatoes to the boiling water for 40 seconds and then cool them in the prepared ice bath. When they are completely cooled, peel (pulling the skin from the edges of the X) and chop the tomatoes, discarding the seeds.

Combine the tomatoes, white wine, and vinegar in a saucepan over low heat and cook, stirring constantly, for 1 hour, or until all of the liquid has evaporated. The mixture should look like a paste. Remove from the heat and cool completely. Once cooled, add the tarragon, chives, and olive oil and whisk to combine. Season with a pinch of salt and pepper and set aside.

In a saucepan over medium heat, bring 3¾ cups chicken stock and the heavy cream to a simmer. Once simmering, add the grits, reduce the heat to low, and add the Parmesan, white cheddar, salt, and pepper, stirring constantly. Continue to cook until the grits are thick and creamy, about 30 minutes. Cover and keep warm.

Soak four bamboo skewers in water. Heat a grill to medium-high heat and oil the grates well. Place six shrimp on each skewer, brush with oil on both sides, and season with salt and pepper to taste. Grill the shrimp for 3 to 4 minutes on each side.

In a sauté pan over medium heat, cook the sliced garlic in 1 tablespoon butter until the garlic softens. Add the chopped kale, 1 tablespoon tomato concassé, and the crushed red pepper and cook for 2 to 3 more minutes. Add ¼ cup chicken stock and cook for 2 minutes more.

Bring 12 cups water and 1 teaspoon distilled vinegar to simmer in a saucepan. Poach the eggs four at a time: 2½ minutes for a soft poach, 4 minutes for medium, and 8 minutes for a hard poach.

To serve, spoon about 1½ cups grits per serving into a shallow, wide-rimmed bowl. Top with the kale and a poached egg. Arrange six shrimp around the egg, and garnish each egg with 1 tablespoon of the concassé tomatoes.

CONCASSÉ TOMATOES WITH OLIVE OIL
Salt
10 Roma tomatoes
1 cup dry white wine
½ cup Champagne vinegar
1 tablespoon chopped tarragon
1 tablespoon chopped chives
2 tablespoons extra virgin olive oil
Black pepper

GRITS
3¾ cups chicken stock
1 cup heavy cream
2½ cups Homestead Gristmill grits
½ cup grated Parmesan cheese
½ cup grated white cheddar cheese
Salt and black pepper

SHRIMP
24 (16/20) shrimp, peeled and
   deveined, tails on
Oil
Salt and black pepper

KALE
2 cloves garlic, thinly sliced
4 tablespoons (½ stick) unsalted
   butter
1 bunch kale, stemmed and roughly
   chopped
1 teaspoon crushed red pepper
¼ cup chicken stock

1 teaspoon distilled vinegar
4 eggs

Mansion on Turtle Creek Granola

SERVES 10 TO 12

Preheat the oven to 325 degrees F.

Combine the oats, nuts, seeds, and coconut flakes in a mixing bowl. Melt the honey, butter, and brown sugar in a small saucepan over low heat. Add the vanilla and stir to blend.

Place the dry ingredients in a roasting pan and pour the melted butter mixture over the top. Toss the mixture to coat it with the butter. Place in the preheated oven and bake for 15 minutes or until golden, stirring every 5 minutes to keep the mixture from burning.

Remove from the oven and set aside to cool. The granola will be soggy at first but will crisp as it cools. Use your hands to break it apart if necessary.

Serve with sliced fresh fruit or berries, and heavy cream or milk.

4 cups rolled oats, uncooked (not instant)
¼ cup sliced almonds
¼ cup chopped unsalted pistachios
⅛ cup pine nuts
¼ cup unsalted sunflower seeds
¼ cup unsalted pumpkin seeds
¼ cup unsweetened coconut flakes
¼ cup honey
2 tablespoons unsalted butter
2 tablespoons light brown sugar
¼ teaspoon pure vanilla extract

GARNISH
Fresh berries
Heavy cream

Huevos Rancheros

SALSA

6 beefsteak tomatoes, halved

3 jalapeños, stemmed and halved lengthwise

1 yellow onion, roughly chopped

5 cloves garlic

1 tablespoon canola oil

½ tablespoon sherry vinegar

Salt

Black pepper

PICO DE GALLO

3 Roma tomatoes, finely diced

½ red onion, finely diced

1 jalapeño, seeded and finely diced

1 tablespoon chopped cilantro

1 teaspoon olive oil

Juice of 1 lime

Salt

Black pepper

GUACAMOLE

1 avocado, halved and pitted

1 teaspoon chopped chives

3 dashes Tabasco sauce

2 teaspoons chopped cilantro

Juice of ½ lemon

Salt

Black pepper

8 eggs

1 cup cooked and crumbled chorizo

4 corn tostadas (fried corn tortillas)

¼ cup sour cream

2 cups cooked black beans

¼ cup jalapeño jack cheese

To make the salsa, preheat the oven to 350 degrees F. In a mixing bowl, combine the tomatoes, jalapeños, onion, garlic, and oil and toss to coat. On a sheet pan lined with parchment paper, place the vegetables in a single layer and bake for 35 to 45 minutes.

Remove the pan from the oven and let the vegetables cool to room temperature. In a food processor fitted with a metal blade, combine the vegetables and vinegar and pulse to a puree. Season with salt and pepper to taste and set aside.

To make the pico de gallo, combine the tomatoes, onion, jalapeño, cilantro, olive oil, and lime juice in a mixing bowl. Season with a pinch of salt and black pepper. Mix well and set aside.

To make the guacamole, scoop the flesh out of the skin of the avocado and place in a mixing bowl. Smash the flesh with a fork. Add the chives, Tabasco, cilantro, and lemon juice. Season the guacamole with salt and pepper as desired. Mix well and set aside.

Heat a nonstick sauté pan over medium heat. Spray with cooking spray and cook the eggs, two at a time, for 4 to 5 minutes on one side to achieve a sunny-side-up egg.

To serve, scoop ¼ cup cooked chorizo in the center of each plate and top with a warm tostada. Top each tostada with two sunny-side-up eggs and garnish with the salsa, pico de gallo, guacamole, and sour cream. Serve with black beans on the side, topped with a tablespoon of pepper jack cheese.

Note: The eggs can be cooked any style that you prefer, such as scrambled or over easy.

Zucchini and Ricotta Cannelloni
with cherry tomatoes

SERVES 4

ZUCCHINI-RICOTTA MIXTURE
2 shallots, minced
5 tablespoons extra virgin olive oil
3 zucchini, finely diced
¼ cup ricotta
Salt and black pepper

MARINATED CHERRY
TOMATOES
12 cherry tomatoes, halved
1¼ red onions, diced
1 tablespoon minced chives
1 tablespoon balsamic vinegar
1 teaspoon crushed red pepper
4 large basil leaves, chopped
Salt and black pepper

8 cannelloni pasta shells

In a sauté pan over low heat, cook the shallots in 1 tablespoon extra virgin olive oil for 5 minutes, or until they are soft and translucent. Add the diced zucchini and cook for 8 minutes, or until soft. Transfer to a mixing bowl and refrigerate for 1 hour. When the mixture is completely cool, mix in the ricotta and season with salt and black pepper to taste. Refrigerate until ready to use.

In a mixing bowl, combine the tomatoes, red onions, chives, 2 tablespoons olive oil, the vinegar, crushed red pepper, basil, and salt and pepper to taste.

Preheat the oven to 350 degrees F. Boil the cannelloni shells in generously salted water for 5 minutes. Cool in an ice bath and pat dry with a paper towel. Using a spoon, stuff the cannelloni shells with the zucchini-ricotta mixture. Place the stuffed shells in a baking dish and brush with 2 tablespoons extra virgin olive oil. Bake for 15 minutes. When warm, broil briefly to brown the tops and remove from the oven.

Serve topped with the marinated cherry tomatoes.

Fire-Roasted Chiles Rellenos
with mushrooms, Spanish rice, and candied pecans

SERVES 4

Preheat the oven to 250 degrees F. In a 2-quart saucepot, bring 1 cup water and 1 cup sugar to a boil. When the sugar has dissolved, add the pecans and bring the pot to a boil once more. Drain the pecans and discard the liquid. Place the pecans on a parchment-lined sheet tray, sprinkle them with the remaining sugar, the cinnamon, and cayenne pepper, and bake for 1 hour, turning once. Remove the pecans from the oven and set aside.

In a large, heavy-bottomed pot over medium heat, cook the rice in the canola oil and 3 tablespoons butter for 10 minutes, stirring constantly. The rice will brown slightly and give off a nutty aroma. Add the dry spices and stir well. Add 4 cups chicken stock and the tomato paste and stir well to combine. Reduce the heat to low, cover, and cook for 8 to 10 minutes, or until all of the liquid has been absorbed. Transfer the rice to a mixing bowl.

In a sauté pan over medium heat, cook the shallots in 3 tablespoons butter until they are translucent. Add the mushrooms and sauté for 5 to 7 minutes. Add ¼ cup chicken stock and continue cooking until all of the liquid has evaporated. Combine with the Spanish rice and season with a pinch of salt and black pepper.

On a well-heated fire grill, roast the peppers 5 minutes on each side to char the skin. Place the peppers in a mixing bowl and cover with plastic wrap. Set aside for 1 hour.

To make the guacamole, scoop the flesh out of the skin of the avocado and place in a mixing bowl. Smash the flesh with a fork. Add the chives, Tabasco, cilantro, and lemon juice. Season the guacamole with salt and pepper as desired. Mix well and set aside.

When cool enough to handle, peel the skin off each pepper. Make a small slit in each pepper to clean out the seeds, keeping the pepper whole. Stuff the peppers with the rice mixture and carefully dredge each pepper in flour seasoned with salt and pepper.

Heat the peanut oil in a sauté pan over medium heat. When the oil begins to shimmer, dip the peppers in the beaten egg and fry for 5 minutes on each side. Transfer the peppers to a baking sheet and bake for 8 minutes.

Serve with guacamole and garnish with candied pecans.

CANDIED TEXAS PECANS
2 cups sugar
1 cup Texas pecan halves
1 tablespoon ground cinnamon
½ teaspoon cayenne pepper

SPANISH RICE
2 cups long-grain rice
¼ cup canola oil
6 tablespoons unsalted butter
1 tablespoon ground cumin
2 tablespoons chili powder
1 tablespoon dried Mexican oregano
1 tablespoon Spanish paprika
1 teaspoon garlic powder
4 ¼ cups chicken stock
2 tablespoons tomato paste
2 shallots, minced
8 ounces field mushrooms, such as chanterelles, morels, and black trumpets, cleaned
Salt and black pepper

4 large poblano peppers
2 cups flour
Salt and black pepper
1 cup peanut oil
6 eggs, beaten

GUACAMOLE
1 avocado, halved and seeded
1 teaspoon chopped chives
3 dashes Tabasco sauce
2 teaspoons chopped cilantro
Juice of ½ lemon
Salt
Black pepper

Foie Gras Doughnuts

SERVES 6

In a 2-quart saucepot over medium heat, cook the port and black peppercorns for 1 hour, or until the mixture has reduced and becomes thick and bubbly. Strain out the peppercorns and reserve the reduction to top the doughnuts.

To make the meringue, combine the sugar and egg whites in the bowl of a standing mixer and mix until soft peaks form.

In a food processor fitted with a metal blade, process the flours, yeast, and salt. Add the beer, egg yolks, canola oil, and cognac and combine. Transfer the mixture to a mixing bowl and fold in the meringue. Transfer the dough to a pastry bag fitted with a tip.

In round molds measuring 1¼ inches in diameter and 1 inch high, pipe ⅓-inch of the dough and freeze for 1 hour (see note). Remove the frozen dough from the freezer and place a piece of the chilled foie gras in each round.

Pipe the remaining dough over the foie gras to cover and fill ¾-inch up the side of the mold. Do not fill the mold all the way to the top. Return the molds to the freezer for 1 hour.

In a 2-quart saucepot, heat the peanut oil to 350 degrees F. Preheat the oven to 400 degrees F.

Remove the frozen doughnut dough from the freezer and remove from the molds. Fry the doughnuts in batches of five for 4 minutes each, turning so that the doughnuts are evenly golden brown in color. Transfer the doughnuts to a sheet tray and bake for 2 to 3 minutes. Remove from the oven and let the doughnuts cool on a paper towel for 8 minutes. Top the doughnuts with the port reduction and serve.

Note: Finding the right molds for these are crucial to the outcome of the doughnuts. If the molds are too big, the center of the doughnut will not cook. If they are too small, the foie gras will melt out into the oil.

BLACK PEPPER–INFUSED PORT REDUCTION
3 cups port
15 black peppercorns

MERINGUE
½ cup sugar
½ cup egg whites

DOUGH
2¼ cups all-purpose flour
¼ cup plus 1½ tablespoons cake flour
2 teaspoons active dry yeast
Pinch salt
1 cup plus 1 tablespoon beer
4 egg yolks
¼ cup canola oil
2 teaspoons cognac
5 ounces chilled foie gras, cut into ¼-inch dice
8 cups peanut oil

Bar Food & Cocktails

Texas Grits Fries

Cod Fritters

Lobster Sliders

Smoked Short Rib Tacos

Fried Oysters

Cham Cham

Simple Syrup

Ginger-Infused Simple Syrup

Moscow Mule

Blazing Turtle

Gingerita

Passion Lily

Mansion-Style Dark and Stormy

Pink Panther

Homemade Tonic with Gin

Mansion Martini

Mansion Coffee

Texas Grits Fries *with chipotle aioli*

SERVES 4

CHIPOTLE AIOLI
1 (7 ½-ounce) can chipotle peppers
5 egg yolks plus 1 whole egg
3 cloves garlic
Juice of 2 limes
3 cups canola oil
Pinch salt

GRITS FRIES
1 cup Homestead Gristmill grits
1 tablespoon olive oil
3 cups chicken stock
Salt
1 teaspoon ancho chile powder
1 teaspoon chili powder
½ teaspoon garlic powder
½ teaspoon onion powder
¼ cup shredded cheddar cheese
¼ cup grated Parmesan cheese
1 cup flour
Black pepper

In a food processor fitted with a metal blade, puree the chipotles. Add the egg yolks, egg, garlic, and lime juice. While the food processor is running, slowly add the oil and season with salt.

Wash the grits in cold water to extract the husk. In a large saucepan over medium heat, toast the grits with 1 tablespoon olive oil for 2 minutes. Add the chicken stock and cook slowly for 30 minutes, stirring often. Add a pinch of salt, both chile powders, the garlic powder, onion powder, and cheeses. Mix well and spread the grits into a 1-inch layer on the bottom of a baking dish. Cover and refrigerate the grits for 1 hour.

Season the flour with salt and pepper and put it in a bowl. When the grits have cooled, invert them onto a cutting board. Cut the grits into 1 x 4-inch pieces. Cut each piece in half lengthwise, and halve it again so the grits resemble French fries. Dredge each fry in the seasoned flour and shake off any excess.

Fry the grits in a saucepot with 3 inches of vegetable oil at 375 degrees F for 5 minutes, or until golden brown. Dry the fries on a paper towel, season with salt, and serve with the chipotle aioli.

Cod Fritters *with spicy tomatillo sauce*

SERVES 4

SPICY TOMATILLO SAUCE
10 tomatillos, husks left on
3 cloves garlic, chopped
1 small red onion, diced
1 jalapeño, seeded, stemmed, and
  diced
2 teaspoons chopped cilantro
1 teaspoon cayenne pepper
1 tablespoon Champagne vinegar
2 tablespoons canola oil
Salt
Black pepper

COD FRITTERS
1 loaf country bread
1 pound Atlantic cod fillet (tell the
  butcher you want the tail end)
4 tablespoons gray sea salt
4 cups whole milk
1 sprig fresh thyme
4 cloves garlic
8 ounces Yukon gold potatoes
2 tablespoons extra virgin olive oil
Salt and black pepper
½ teaspoon cayenne pepper
2 egg yolks
1 tablespoon chopped Italian parsley
2 cups grapeseed oil

To make the tomatillo sauce, preheat the oven to 350 degrees F. Place the tomatillos on a sheet tray and roast them for 12 to 15 minutes. Remove them from the oven and set aside to cool. When they are cool enough to handle, remove the husks and cores. In a food processor fitted with a metal blade, combine the tomatillos, garlic, onion, jalapeño, cilantro, cayenne, vinegar, and oil. Pulse for a few seconds, or until all the ingredients are well incorporated. Season the sauce with salt and black pepper to taste, transfer to a serving dish, and set aside.

To make the bread crumbs, preheat the oven to 250 degrees F. Cut the crust from the country bread and discard. Cut or tear the bread into small pieces. Place the pieces on a sheet tray and bake for 1 hour, stirring the bread pieces to turn after the first half hour. Transfer the dried bread to a food processor and pulse until crumbs are formed. Set aside.

Cover the cod fillet with the sea salt. Allow the fish to rest for 7 minutes, then wash off the salt. Pat the fillet dry with a paper towel.

In a 2-quart saucepan, bring the whole milk, thyme, and garlic to a simmer. Add the cod fillet to the milk (if it does not fit in the pot, cut the fillet in half) and cook over low heat for 12 to 15 minutes, or until the cod flakes with a fork. Strain the fish in a colander and discard the thyme and garlic. Cool the cod in the refrigerator for 30 minutes.

Cover the potatoes with water in a large saucepot and bring them to a simmer. Cook the potatoes for 1 hour, or until they are soft when pierced with a knife. Drain the potatoes. When they are cool enough to handle, peel the potatoes and transfer them to a medium mixing bowl. Add the olive oil and mash the potatoes with a fork. Season well with salt and pepper. Add the cod, cayenne, egg yolks, and chopped parsley and mix well to combine. Roll the mixture into bite-size balls, and then roll the balls in the bread crumbs.

In a 2-quart saucepan, heat the grapeseed oil to 360 degrees F. Fry the breaded cod balls in batches of six for 5 minutes, or until golden brown. Remove the fritters with a slotted spoon and place them on paper towels to drain. Serve with tomatillo sauce.

Lobster Sliders *with tarragon aioli*

SERVES 6

CONFIT TOMATOES
Salt
4 Roma tomatoes
5 cloves garlic
1 sprig thyme
2 tablespoons olive oil

TARRAGON AIOLI
3 cloves garlic
1 tablespoon extra virgin olive oil
½ cup mayonnaise (made with
    grapeseed oil)
1 teaspoon tarragon mustard
1 bunch tarragon, stemmed and
    chopped
1 bunch chives, minced
Zest and juice of 1 lemon
Pinch cayenne pepper
Salt and black pepper

SLIDERS
5 (U10) sea scallops
¼ cup heavy cream
2 ½ pounds cooked lobster meat
Salt and black pepper
Juice of ½ lemon
Zest of 1 lemon
3 tablespoons extra virgin olive oil
4 (2-inch) brioche buns
1 bunch watercress
½ bunch dill, stemmed and chopped

POTATO CRISPS
(page 24)
Lemon salt

To make the confit tomatoes, preheat the oven to 225 degrees F. Bring 4 quarts salted water to a boil. Prepare 4 quarts ice water in a large mixing bowl. Make a small X on the bottom of each tomato with a sharp knife. Add the tomatoes to the boiling water for 40 seconds, then allow them to cool in the prepared ice bath.

When completely cooled, peel the tomatoes by pulling up the edges of the X, then quarter the tomatoes. Toss the quarters in a medium mixing bowl with the garlic, thyme, and olive oil. Place the tomatoes on a parchment-lined sheet tray and bake for 1 hour, turning every 20 minutes. Remove the tomatoes from the oven and set aside.

To make the tarragon aioli, heat the garlic in the extra virgin olive oil in a sauté pan over low heat until for 2 minutes, or until tender. Remove the garlic from the pan, allow it to cool, and crush it. In a mixing bowl, combine the mayonnaise, crushed garlic, tarragon mustard, chopped tarragon, minced chives, lemon juice, zest, and cayenne pepper. Season with salt and pepper and set aside until ready to serve.

To make the lobster sliders, place the scallops in a food processor fitted with a metal blade and puree until smooth. Transfer the scallops to a bowl and add the heavy cream. Fold the scallop mixture into the lobster meat and season with salt, pepper, lemon juice, and lemon zest. Form the meat into four lightly packed patties and keep them cold until you are ready to cook them.

In a nonstick sauté pan over medium heat, sear the patties in extra virgin olive oil for 3 minutes on each side, or until golden brown. Split the brioche buns, sprinkle them with olive oil, and lightly toast them.

Place a lobster patty on the bottom of each brioche bun and top with the tarragon aioli, confit tomatoes, and watercress. Cover with the top of the bun. Serve with crispy potato chips and season with dill and lemon salt.

Smoked Short Rib Tacos

SERVES 4

To make the mayonnaise, combine the peppers and mayonnaise in a blender and blend to incorporate. Season with salt and pepper to taste, transfer to a bowl, and cover. Refrigerate until ready to serve.

To smoke the ribs, preheat a smoker with hickory wood chips. If you do not have a smoker, soak the hickory wood chips in water for 2 hours. Remove the grates of your grill, place 3 sheets of aluminum foil over the heat source, and place the soaked chips over the foil. Replace the grates, place a fine-mesh screen over the grates, and place the meat on top. Close the lid of the grill or smoker and smoke the ribs for 15 minutes.

While the meat is smoking, assemble the slaw for the tacos. In a small mixing bowl, combine the cabbage, red onion, and carrot. Season with lemon juice, salt, and pepper to taste and set aside.

In a medium sauté pan over medium heat, heat the smoked short ribs and the caramelized onions. Grill the tortillas over medium heat just long enough to heat them through.

Place two heated tortillas on each of four small plates. Divide the meat among the tortillas, then divide the slaw over the meat. Add a dollop of the chipotle mayonnaise, then garnish with the lime wedges and cilantro to serve.

CHIPOTLE MAYONNAISE
1 (7 ½-ounce) can chipotle peppers
1 cup mayonnaise
Salt
Black pepper

TACOS
3 cups hickory wood chips, soaked
1 pound cooked beef short ribs
  (page 87)

SLAW
1 cup shredded green cabbage
1 cup shredded red cabbage
1 red onion, halved and thinly sliced
1 carrot, peeled and cut into thin
  strips
Juice of 1 lemon
Salt and black pepper

½ cup caramelized onions
8 (6-inch) flour tortillas
8 lime wedges, for garnish
Fresh cilantro, for garnish

Fried Oysters *with tartar sauce and dill*

SERVES 4

To make the tartar sauce, combine the egg yolks, mustard, and canola oil in a blender and process for 2 minutes, or until it thickens to a mayonnaise texture. Transfer to a mixing bowl and add the onion, cornichon, lemon juice and zest, parsley, capers, and hot sauce. Season with salt to taste. Cover and reserve in the refrigerator until ready to serve.

Heat enough oil for frying in a pot over medium heat to 360 degrees F.

Pat the oysters dry with a paper towel. Place the flour, eggs, and bread crumbs each in three separate bowls. Whisk the eggs and season them with salt and black pepper. Toss chives into the bread crumbs.

Dip the oysters, one at a time, in the flour, followed by the egg, and then into the bread crumbs. Repeat this process until all the oysters are coated.

Fry the breaded oysters in hot oil four at a time for 4 minutes, or until golden brown. Drain on a paper towel.

To serve, place the fried oysters back in their cleaned shells and top with a dollop of tartar sauce and a sprig of fresh dill.

TARTAR SAUCE
3 egg yolks
1 tablespoon Dijon mustard
2 cups canola oil
1 tablespoon minced red onion
2 tablespoons chopped cornichon
   (gherkin)
Juice and zest of 1 lemon
2 tablespoons chopped Italian parsley
1 tablespoon capers, chopped
1 teaspoon hot sauce
Salt

OYSTERS
1 quart canola oil for frying
16 medium oysters, shucked, shells
   reserved
2 cups all-purpose flour
4 eggs
2 cups panko (Japanese bread crumbs)
Salt and black pepper
2 tablespoons chopped fresh chives
2 tablespoons fresh dill

Cocktails in the
library bar, from left:
Gingerita
Pink Panther
Cham Cham
Homemade Tonic
with Gin
Mansion-Style Dark
and Stormy
Blazing Turtle

Cham Cham

SERVES 1

½ ounce Chambord
5 ounces Champagne
Fresh raspberries, for garnish

Pour the Chambord into a chilled Champagne flute and top with the Champagne. Garnish with a skewer of fresh raspberries across the top of the glass to serve.

Simple Syrup

YIELDS 2 CUPS

2 cups granulated sugar

Combine the sugar and 2 cups water in a saucepan, stir, and bring to a boil. Reduce the heat to low and simmer for 15 minutes, stirring occasionally. Allow the syrup to cool and store in a covered container or a bottle in the refrigerator for up to 1 month.

Ginger-Infused Simple Syrup

YIELDS 3 CUPS

2 cups granulated sugar
1 cup peeled and sliced ginger

Combine the sugar and 3 cups water in a saucepan, stir, and bring to a boil. Reduce the heat to low, add the ginger, and allow the syrup to simmer for 15 minutes, stirring occasionally. Allow the syrup to cool, and store in the refrigerator for up to 1 month.

Moscow Mule

SERVES 1

2 ounces vodka
½ ounce fresh lime juice
½ ounce simple syrup (page 214)
3 ounces ginger beer
Lime wedge, for garnish

This is the drink that introduced vodka to the American palate. At the Mansion it's special because it's made with our homemade ginger beer. The presentation is special too—it's served in a traditional copper mug.

Fill a chilled copper mug with ice and add the vodka, lime juice, simple syrup, and ginger beer, in that order. Stir and garnish with a lime wedge to serve.

Blazing Turtle

SERVES 1

½ ounce peach puree (found in frozen section of grocery)
¼ ounce ginger-infused simple syrup (page 214)
½ ounce Lillet Blonde
3 ounces Champagne
Pinch ancho chile powder, for garnish

Combine the peach puree, simple syrup, and Lillet Blonde in a shaker filled with ice and shake until chilled. Pour into a chilled martini glass and top with the Champagne. Garnish with a pinch of ancho chile on top and serve.

Gingerita

Combine all of the ingredients in a shaker filled with ice and shake vigorously until chilled and frothy. Strain into a rocks glass filled with ice. Garnish with a lime wedge to serve.

1 ounce fresh lime juice
½ ounce ginger-infused syrup (page 214)
1 egg white
1 ½ ounces tequila
¼ ounce Cointreau
Lime wedge, for garnish

Passion Lily

SERVES 1

Combine all of the ingredients in a shaker filled with ice and shake until cold. Strain into a chilled martini glass and garnish with an edible flower.

1½ ounces vodka
½ ounce St. Germain
½ ounce fresh lime juice
¾ ounce cranberry juice
Edible flower, for garnish

Mansion-Style Dark and Stormy

SERVES 1

Coat the bottom of a rocks glass with falernum and top with ice. Add the ginger beer and float the rum on top of the ginger beer. Garnish with a lime wedge to serve.

   Note: Falernum is a sweet syrup used to make Caribbean and tropical mixed drinks. It can be found online.

½ ounce falernum (see note)
3 ounces ginger beer
1½ ounces rum
Lime wedge, for garnish

 This great summer drink is one of the bartender's favorites, and he says that with good quality ingredients it has the capability to be greater than the sum of its parts. At the Mansion, it features Ron Zacapa rum and our house-made falernum and ginger beer. But the bartender recommends John D. Taylor's Velvet Falernum and a good ginger beer from a specialty store. *Do not* substitute ginger ale.

Pink Panther

SERVES 4

WATERMELON-VODKA INFUSION
1 small seedless watermelon
1 liter vodka

2 ounces watermelon-vodka infusion
6 to 8 fresh mint leaves
¾ ounce fresh lemon juice
¾ ounce simple syrup (page 214)

To make the infusion, peel and cube the watermelon and process it in a blender until pureed and smooth. Pour the puree into a large glass jar with a lid and add the vodka. Allow the infusion to steep in the refrigerator for 1 week, stirring every other day, as the mixture will separate.

To make the Pink Panther, pour 2 ounces of the watermelon-vodka infusion into a shaker glass, add mint leaves, and muddle to release the mint oils. Add the lemon juice and simple syrup, top with ice, and shake. Strain into a chilled cocktail glass and garnish with fresh mint leaves.

This has been a very popular summer drink at the Mansion Bar, especially with women. The idea was to take simple summer flavors and make a refreshing drink—hence the watermelon, mint, and lemon.

THE MANSION ON TURTLE CREEK

Homemade Tonic with Gin

¾ ounce fresh lime juice
½ ounce simple syrup (page 214)
1½ ounces gin
Very small pinch quinine powder
2½ ounces sparkling water
Lime wedge, for garnish

Build the drink in a Collins glass. Fill the glass with ice and add the lime juice and simple syrup. Add the gin and quinine powder and top with the sparkling water. Stir to combine and garnish with a lime wedge to serve.

Quinine power, derived from cinchona tree bark and originally used to treat malaria, is what makes this drink so special and gives it that "wow" factor. But a word of warning: It is easy to kill this drink because quinine is very bitter. In the Mansion Bar we use ¹/₁₆ of a bar spoon—it takes very little.

Mansion Martini

2 ounces vodka
¾ ounce Chambord
1½ ounces Champagne
Lime wedge, for garnish

Combine the vodka and Chambord in a shaker filled with ice and shake until chilled. Pour into a chilled martini glass and top with the Champagne. Garnish with a lime wedge to serve.

Mansion Coffee

½ ounce amaretto
½ ounce Kahlúa
½ ounce Baileys Irish Cream
½ ounce brandy
6 ounces hot coffee
Sweetened whipped cream, for
  garnish (optional)

Combine all of the ingredients in a coffee mug and stir to combine. Top with sweetened whipped cream if desired and serve.

The Wine of Texas / BECKER VINEYARDS

RICHARD BECKER has always had confidence in his own opinion, even when it goes against conventional theory. You might even call Becker a contrarian. When the San Antonio–based endocrinologist and his wife, Bunny, found a weekend home in the Texas Hill Country in the early 1990s, the fact that it was located between two wineries suggested the notion that they, too, could have a winery. But proximity wasn't proof enough for the skeptical Becker that his grapes would produce a decent wine. "I liked local wines then," the doctor admits. "At the time, though, the general bias was toward sweetness." But the Beckers were intrigued by the possibilities: Bunny is a skilled cook, and Richard was fascinated by wines. Together they had developed an obsession with wine and food pairings. So, with only a firm sense of what they liked—and no evidence that Texas palates could be nudged off the sweet end of the spectrum—the Beckers began to grow grapes in their vineyard near Stonewall in 1992. The vineyard was planted on a site of native Mustang grapes highly prized for winemaking by the Beckers' German neighbors and their ancestors.

By the time Richard and Bunny had their first harvest in 1995, American tastes in wine were changing. Although the two were producing wines that suited their own taste buds, enthusiasts recognized the veracity of their point of view. The Mansion on Turtle Creek was one of the first to notice. "We hadn't even started marketing our product," says Richard, "when Dean Fearing added four of our wines to his menu." A high point for the vineyards came when Fearing celebrated The Mansion's quarter-century birthday with a big dinner at the restaurant and poured Becker Vineyards' Reserve Chardonnay. Today, The Mansion's 700-label wine list still includes offerings from Becker Vineyards—the only Texas winery singled out for inclusion.

Most vintages are aged in new French oak, others in new American oak—all are stored in the largest underground wine cellar in Texas (so, yes, bigger is better in this case). That first year Becker Vineyards produced 1,500 cases of wine. In 2011 output was 100,000 cases. The 46 acres of French Vinifera vines generate eight different available varietals, including Syrah, Petite Syrah, Sauvignon Blanc, Malbec, Petite Verdot, Cabernet Sauvignon, Cabernet Franc, and Merlot. The Beckers continue to experiment: "We were the first in Texas to plant Viognier grapes," notes Bunny. That was when there were only about 70 acres in the United States that were growing the grape. "At the time we thought no one would know what it was." But the Beckers' instinct again proved unerring, if not prescient. "I think Viognier may become the white wine of Texas," predicts Bunny.

Desserts

Peach Sundae

Ruby Red Grapefruit Tart

Hazelnut, Chocolate, and Caramel Napoleon

Spiced Mexican Chocolate Custard with Churros

Seven-Layer Chocolate Torte

Turtle Creek Pie

Vanilla Crème Brûlée with Rasperry Maramalade

Lemon Pie

Goat Cheese Cheesecake with Berry Compote

Peach Sundae
with Champagne sabayon and red currants

SERVES 4

PEACH SORBET
3 peaches, peeled, pitted,
 and chopped
⅓ cup sugar

POACHED PEACHES
4 peaches
1 cup sugar
2 tablespoons honey
1 sprig thyme
Zest of 1 orange
1 vanilla bean, split and scraped

VANILLA PANNA COTTA
1½ cups heavy cream
⅔ cup sugar
2 tablespoons powdered gelatin
1 ⅔ cups plain yogurt
¼ sour cream

CHAMPAGNE SABAYON
3 egg yolks
3 tablespoons sugar
¼ cup Champagne

RED CURRANTS
⅓ cup sugar
¾ cup red currants

¼ cup sliced almonds, toasted

To make the peach sorbet, process the chopped peaches in a food processor to achieve a fine puree. Pass the puree through a strainer. Combine the sugar with ½ cup water in a pot over medium heat and bring to a boil. Add 1 cup of the peach puree, remove from the heat, and allow the mixture to cool. Process in an ice cream freezer according to the manufacturer's instructions.

To poach the peaches, first stem them, and use a paring knife to score them each with an X on the bottom. Whisk 2 cups water with the sugar, honey, thyme, orange peel, and vanilla bean in a medium saucepan. Put the stemmed, scored peaches in the saucepan with the liquid and gently place a circle of parchment paper over the top of the liquid to create a light barrier between the peaches and the air. Bring to a boil over high heat. Once the liquid reaches a boil, remove the pot from the heat and set aside, allowing the peaches to cool in the liquid. After the liquid has cooled, remove the peaches and peel off the skin, starting at the bottom and pulling upwards from the edges of the scored X. Pour the poaching liquid into a plastic container, put the skinned peaches back into the liquid, cover, and refrigerate until ready to use. They will keep for 1 week stored in an airtight container in the refrigerator.

Prepare the vanilla panna cotta by bringing the cream and the sugar to a boil over medium heat in a small saucepan. Meanwhile, bloom the gelatin in ½ cup cold water, allowing it to sit for 5 to 10 minutes. Once the cream has boiled, remove it from the heat and let it stand for 1 minute. Strain the gelatin and add it to the cream mixture, whisking to combine, then add the yogurt and sour cream. Pour the panna cotta into four sundae cups and refrigerate until set, at least 6 hours.

To make the Champagne sabayon, fill a medium saucepan one third full of water and place over medium heat. Combine the egg yolks, sugar, and Champagne in a stainless-steel bowl and place the bowl on top of the saucepan to create a double boiler. Whisk the sabayon constantly until it has doubled in volume, 4 to 5 minutes. A ribbon should form when the whisk is lifted out of the sabayon.

To make the red currants, bring ⅜ cup water and the sugar to a boil in a small saucepan over high heat. Once the syrup has boiled, remove the pan from the heat and add the red currants. Set the pan aside to cool.

To serve, pit and slice the poached peaches. Top the panna cotta with a scoop of peach sorbet. Garnish each sundae with poached peaches and drizzle with red currants and Champagne sabayon. Sprinkle with toasted almonds, if using.

Ruby Red Grapefruit Tart
and avocado ice cream

YIELDS 2 TARTS

To make the sweet dough, place the flours, salt, sugar, and zest in a mixer fitted with a paddle attachment. Add the cold, cubed butter on top of the dry ingredients and mix on low speed until the butter is roughly the size of peas. Add the eggs and continue mixing just until the dough comes together. Turn the dough out onto a lightly floured surface and knead to ensure that all the dry ingredients are incorporated. Divide the dough into 2 equal portions, shape each portion into a disc, wrap the discs individually in plastic wrap, and refrigerate for a minimum of 2 hours.

Butter two 10-inch tart pans, or spray them with nonstick spray. After the dough has rested in the refrigerator, remove it from the plastic wrap and roll it out on a lightly floured surface to ⅛-inch thick. The dough should be about 12 inches in diameter. Fold the dough in half horizontally, then fold in half again vertically. Gently place the dough into the tart pan, with the closed edge of the tart positioned in the center of the tart pan. Unfold the dough so that it covers the tart pan entirely. To make sure that the dough fills the tart pan, gently lift the excess dough on the outside of the pan and press it lightly into the corner of the pan. Continue this process around the entire edge of the dough. Next, roll a rolling pin over the top of the tart pan to cut off the excess dough on the outside of the pan. Using a fork, prick holes over the entire bottom of the tart dough in the pan. Repeat this process with the second portion of dough and freeze both tart pans at least 30 minutes prior to baking.

Preheat the oven to 375 degrees F. Line each tart with parchment paper and fill with pie weights. Bake on a baking sheet on the center rack of the oven for 20 to 25 minutes. Remove the shells from the oven and remove the parchment and pie weights. Return the shells to the oven for an additional 10 to 15 minutes, or until the crust has reached an even, golden-brown color. (If necessary, fit a ring of aluminum foil around the edge to prevent burning.) Remove the tart shells from the oven and allow to cool to room temperature.

To make the grapefruit curd, combine the grapefruit juice, eggs, egg yolks, sugar, and zest in saucepan over low heat and whisk lightly to combine. Heat to a boil, whisking constantly to avoid burning, and cook the mixture for 10 minutes or until the curd thickens. Remove from the heat. *(Continued on page 234)*

SWEET DOUGH
1½ cups all-purpose flour
1½ cups cake flour
¼ teaspoon salt
¾ cup sugar
Zest of ½ grapefruit
1 cup (2 sticks) unsalted butter, chilled and cut in ½-inch cubes
2 eggs

GRAPEFRUIT CURD
1 cup fresh grapefruit juice
3 whole eggs
8 egg yolks
¾ cup sugar
Zest of 1 grapefruit
2 tablespoons gelatin
6 tablespoons unsalted butter

AVOCADO ICE CREAM
3 medium-size ripe avocados
½ cup sugar
¾ cup sour cream
1 tablespoon fresh lime juice
⅛ teaspoon salt
½ cup heavy cream

GARNISH
8 grapefruit, peeled and supremed

233
DESSERTS

(Ruby Red Grapefruit Tart, continued)

Sprinkle the gelatin over ½ cup cold water and allow it to bloom for 5 minutes. When the gelatin has bloomed, strain it and add it to the hot curd. Add the butter to the curd in quarters, whisking until the curd is smooth. Divide the curd into two equal portions and fill the two tart shells with one portion each. Place the tarts in the refrigerator to allow the curd to set for at least 1 hour.

Halve the avocados and remove and discard the pits, then remove the skins and place the meat in a food processor (or use a blender), then add the remaining ice cream ingredients. Process or blend the mixture until it is smooth. Follow the directions of your ice cream maker to make the ice cream.

To assemble, remove the chilled tarts from the tart pans and top with the grapefruit sections. Cut each into 8 equal pieces. Serve with a scoop of avocado ice cream.

THE MANSION ON TURTLE CREEK

Hazelnut, Chocolate, and Caramel Napoleon

SERVES 4

2 sheets puff pastry

NUTELLA CREAM
½ cup Nutella (chocolate hazelnut
    spread)
1 cup heavy cream

CARAMEL CREAM
1 teaspoon powdered gelatin
¾ cup sugar
1 whole vanilla bean
½ cup cream
1 cup milk
3 egg yolks
5 teaspoons cornstarch
10 tablespoons unsalted butter,
    at room temperature
Pinch salt

Powdered sugar, for garnish

Preheat the oven to 350 degrees F.

Line a cookie sheet with parchment paper. Place 1 sheet of puff pastry on the parchment, then cover with another sheet of parchment paper. Repeat the same procedure using the second sheet of puff pastry. Bake the pastry for 10 minutes. Remove the cookie sheet from the oven and, using a kitchen towel or hot pad, gently press down on top of the puff pastry to flatten it. Remove the top layer of the parchment and place the puff pastry back in the oven for 7 minutes, or until it turns golden brown on top. Remove the pastry from the oven and set aside.

To prepare the Nutella cream, whip the Nutella and the heavy cream in a stand mixer or with a hand mixer until stiff peaks form. Be careful not to overwhip, as this will make the cream grainy. Place the cream in a bowl, cover, and store in the refrigerator.

To make the caramel cream, mix the gelatin in ½ cup cold water and allow it to sit for 5 to 10 minutes to allow it to bloom.

Place ½ cup sugar and 1½ tablespoons water in a pot over high heat. Cook until the sugar turns a light caramel color.

While the sugar is cooking, split and scrape the vanilla bean and place it in a microwave-safe container along with the cream. Warm the cream and vanilla in the microwave for 1 minute.

When the sugar has reached a light caramel color, remove the pan from the heat and add the warm cream, pouring the cream in slowly so as not to splatter the hot caramel. Whisk the milk into the hot caramel mixture and set aside.

Combine the egg yolks, ¼ cup sugar, and the cornstarch in a metal, non-reactive bowl and whisk together until well blended. Add the hot caramel mixture to the egg yolks a little at a time to temper the mixture, taking care to avoid splattering. Return the caramel cream mixture to a saucepan over medium heat. Bring the mixture back to a boil, whisking constantly to avoid scorching, for 3 minutes, or until the caramel cream thickens. Remove it from the heat. Drain the bloomed gelatin and stir it into the caramel cream. Strain this mixture into a metal bowl, cover, and set aside until the caramel cream cools to 104 degrees F.

When the the caramel cream has cooled sufficiently, add the butter using an immersion blender and adding small pieces of the butter at a time until they are fully incorporated. Blend in the salt. When the caramel cream is smooth, place it in a bowl, cover tightly, and store it in the refrigerator.

To assemble the napoleon, cut the puff pastry into rectangles as desired. You can make one large napoleon for a family-style presentation, or you can cut the puff pastry into individually sized portions—just make sure that you have three pieces of equal size for each individual serving in order to layer the dessert properly.

Place the caramel cream and the Nutella cream in two separate piping bags fitted with similarly sized tips. Take one sheet of the puff pastry and pipe cylinders of the caramel cream on top, piping from one corner to another, until you have covered the entire surface of the pastry. Place one of the remaining pieces of puff pastry on top of the caramel cream. Pipe the Nutella cream on top of this layer of puff pastry, in the same fashion as the caramel cream. Place the last piece of puff pastry on top of the Nutella cream. Sprinkle the top of the napoleon with powdered sugar, transfer to a plate, and serve.

Spiced Mexican Chocolate Custard with Churros

SPICED MEXICAN CHOCOLATE CUSTARD

1½ cups heavy cream
6 tablespoons whole milk
2 tablespoons sugar
1 egg yolk
⅛ teaspoon ground cinnamon
⅛ teaspoon instant espresso powder
Small pinch chile powder
1 vanilla bean, split and scraped
Pinch salt
6 ounces dark chocolate, chopped
Cocoa powder, for garnish

CHURROS

(Yields 8)
½ cup milk
Pinch salt
Pinch sugar
1 cup all-purpose flour
1 to 2 egg whites
8 cups oil, for frying

CINNAMON-SUGAR COATING

½ cup sugar
1½ teaspoons ground cinnamon

To make the custard, combine the cream, milk, sugar, egg yolk, cinnamon, espresso powder, chile powder, vanilla bean, and salt in a saucepan over medium heat and bring the mixture to 175 degrees F (just before it begins to simmer), whisking constantly. Remove the pan from the heat and add the chocolate. Mix with an immersion blender, or whisk to combine. Strain the custard into a metal nonreactive bowl and place the bowl in an ice bath until the custard has cooled. Pour the custard evenly into 6-ounce ramekins. Wrap the ramekins with plastic wrap and place in the refrigerator for at least 4 hours to set.

To make the churros, combine ½ cup water, the milk, salt, and sugar in a medium saucepan over medium heat and bring the mixture to a boil. When the mixture begins to boil, remove from the heat and add the flour, stirring constantly until it is fully incorporated. Place the dough in a mixer fitted with a paddle attachment and run the mixer on low to allow the dough to cool. Once the dough has cooled, add the egg whites in several portions in order to loosen up the dough. (Adjust the egg white quantity as needed in order to loosen the dough to a pipeable consistency.) Place the dough in a piping bag fitted with a star tip, line a sheet pan or cookie sheet with parchment paper, and pipe lines of dough in 3½-inch lengths onto the parchment paper. This can be done ahead of time and the churros can be stored in the freezer for up to 2 weeks.

Just before serving, heat the oil to 375 degrees F. Combine the sugar and cinnamon in a shallow bowl. Being careful not to crowd the fryer, fry the churros for 3 to 4 minutes, or until they are golden brown. Remove from the fryer, blot dry with paper towels, then dredge in the cinnamon-sugar mixture.

Take the ramekins from the refrigerator and remove the plastic wrap. Dust the tops of the custard with the cocoa powder and serve with warm churros on the side.

Seven-Layer Chocolate Torte
with cinnamon-vanilla sauce

SERVES 8 TO 10

CHOCOLATE FLOURLESS SPONGE
6½ ounces dark chocolate, chopped
12 tablespoons (¾ cup butter
17 egg yolks
1 cup sugar
17 egg whites

CHOCOLATE GANACHE
1¾ cups heavy cream
⅓ cup sugar
7 tablespoons unsalted butter
10 ounces dark chocolate, chopped

CHOCOLATE MOUSSE
½ cup plus 2 tablespoons milk
2½ cups heavy cream
9 egg yolks
3 tablespoons sugar
1 pound chocolate, chopped

CHOCOLATE GLAZE
⅔ cup heavy cream
1 cup sugar
1 tablespoon powdered gelatin
½ cup cocoa powder

VANILLA-CINNAMON SAUCE
2 cups heavy cream
1 vanilla bean, split and scraped
⅛ teaspoon ground cinnamon
6 egg yolks
¾ cup sugar

To prepare the flourless sponge, preheat the oven to 375 degrees F. Prepare two 10-inch round cake pans by spraying the inside with nonstick spray, then placing a circle of parchment paper on the bottom of each pan.

Combine the chocolate and the butter in a microwave-safe dish. Microwave on medium in 45-second intervals, stirring after each interval, until the chocolate and butter are melted.

Place the egg yolks and ½ cup plus 1 teaspoon sugar in the bowl of a mixer fitted with a whisk attachment. Beat the yolks on high speed until they are light in color and a ribbon forms when the whisk is pulled from the yolk mixture. Turn the mixer to low speed and slowly add the chocolate-butter mixture to the yolks. Once all the chocolate is added, turn the mixer back to high speed and beat for 2 minutes.

Place the egg whites in a separate mixing bowl and whisk on high speed until the whites have doubled in volume. Turn the mixer to low speed and slowly add the remaining sugar. Once all the sugar is added, turn the mixer back to high speed and whip until the meringue forms stiff peaks. Carefully fold the meringue into the chocolate mixture.

Divide the batter evenly between the two cake pans. Bake for 25 minutes, or until the cake springs back when lightly pressed in the middle. Turn the cakes out onto a rack and allow them to cool.

To make the chocolate ganache, combine the cream, sugar, and butter in a medium saucepan and bring the mixture to a boil. Remove the pan from the heat and add the chopped chocolate, stirring constantly until the chocolate has melted. Cover the mixture and allow it to cool to room temperature.

Make the chocolate mousse by combining the milk and ½ cup plus 2 tablespoons cream in a small saucepan. Bring the mixture to a boil over medium heat. In a stainless-steel bowl, whisk together the egg yolks and sugar until they are evenly combined. Temper the cream into the yolks by adding the cream to the yolk mixture in three parts, whisking thoroughly between each addition. Pour the mixture back into the saucepan and bring the mixture to 170 degrees F. Add the chocolate, stirring until the chocolate has melted and the mixture is smooth.

In a mixer fitted with a whisk attachment, whip the remaining cream to soft peaks. Fold one third of the whipped cream into the chocolate mixture, making sure the cream is fully incorporated. Slowly add the chocolate mixture back into the remaining whipped cream, folding it in slowly until the mixture is smooth. Cover and set aside.

To make the chocolate glaze, bring 2 tablespoons water, the cream, and sugar to a boil in a medium saucepan over high heat. Meanwhile, bloom the gelatin in ½ cup cold water, allowing it to sit for 5 to 10 minutes. When the cream mixture has reached a full boil, remove it from the heat and slowly add the cocoa powder, whisking to combine. After the cocoa powder is incorporated, drain the bloomed gelatin and add it to the mixture, whisking thoroughly or using an immersion blender to remove all lumps. Strain the mixture, cover, and set it aside in a warm place.

Make the vanilla-cinnamon sauce by bringing the cream, vanilla bean, and cinnamon to a boil over medium heat in a small saucepan. (The vanilla bean continues to add flavor the longer it sits in the sauce, so leave it in.)

In a separate bowl, combine the egg yolks and sugar. Temper the egg yolks by adding the vanilla cream mixture in four parts, whisking thoroughly between each addition. Place the mixture back in the saucepan and cook over medium-low heat, stirring constantly with a spatula, until the mixture has reached 180 degrees F. Remove the sauce from the heat and chill the pan over an ice water bath.

To assemble the torte, remove the chocolate cakes from the pans. Using a serrated knife, horizontally split each cake into two equal layers. Place the first layer back in a cake pan, then spread half of the mousse on top. Spread the mousse out with an offset spatula (one with a blade that bends up at the handle) and place the next layer of the cake on top of the mousse. Spread all of the ganache over this layer. Set the third layer of cake on top of the ganache and press down gently. Spread the remaining half of mousse on top of this layer and spread evenly with an offset spatula. Cap the torte off with the fourth layer of chocolate cake. Press down gently to even the cake out. Place the cake in the freezer for 20 to 30 minutes to set.

Remove the cake from the freezer, run a paring knife around the edges, and invert the cake over a cooling rack. Pour the glaze all around the edges of the cake first, finishing in the center. Take an offset spatula and gently smooth out the glaze, working from one side to the other. Place the cake in the refrigerator for at least 1 hour to allow the glaze to set. Serve each slice of cake with ¼ cup of the vanilla-cinnamon sauce.

Turtle Creek Pie

Preheat the oven to 350 degrees F.

Combine the eggs and sugar, mixing until the sugar is completely dissolved. Stir in the corn syrup, butter, and vanilla. Strain and set this aside.

Layer the apple slices slanting in one direction on the bottom of the pie crust to form a circle around the outside edge of the shell. Make a second circle of apples inside the first, slanting the slices in the opposite direction. Repeat this process and layer until all the slices are used. Slowly and carefully, pour the filling over the apples. Sprinkle pecans evenly over the top of the filling.

Bake for 1 hour. If the edges of the pie have become too brown during baking, remove the pie from the oven and shield the crust with a ring of foil. Return the pie to the oven and bake for an additional 20 to 25 minutes or until the filling has set. Allow the pie to cool slightly before cutting. Serve with vanilla ice cream if you like.

3 extra large eggs
1 cup sugar
1 cup dark corn syrup
2 tablespoons unsalted butter, melted
1 teaspoon vanilla extract
4 Granny Smith apples, peeled, cored, and thinly sliced
1 pie crust (page 245)
½ cup pecan pieces

Vanilla ice cream (optional)

Vanilla Crème Brûlée
with raspberry marmalade

SERVES 6

RASPBERRY MARMALADE
16 ounces fresh raspberries
1 tablespoon fresh lemon juice
½ cup sugar
1 tablespoon powdered gelatin

VANILLA CRÈME BRÛLÉE
⅞ cup milk
3 ⅜ cups heavy cream
1 vanilla bean, split and scraped
1 ¾ cups sugar
10 egg yolks

To make the marmalade, process the raspberries and lemon juice in a food processor until the berries have liquified. Place the liquid in a microwave-safe bowl, add the sugar, and microwave in 1-minute intervals, stirring after each, until the sugar has dissolved. Bloom the gelatin powder in ¼ cup cold water by sprinkling the gelatin granules over the top of the water. Allow the gelatin to sit for 5 to 10 minutes. Once the gelatin has bloomed, strain it and add it to the raspberry mixture and stir to combine. Coat the bottom of each of six 8-ounce ramekins with a thin layer of marmalade. Refrigerate the ramekins to allow the marmalade to set.

To make the crème brûlée base, combine the milk, cream, and vanilla bean in a saucepan. Bring the cream mixture to a boil, then remove from the heat, cover the pot with plastic wrap, and let it sit for 10 minutes. Remove and discard the vanilla bean. Combine 1 cup sugar and the egg yolks in a medium-sized bowl and whisk to combine. Temper the egg yolks by adding the cream mixture in four parts, whisking thoroughly between each addition.

Preheat the oven to 325 degrees F. Remove the ramekins from the refrigerator, place them in a large cake pan or medium roasting pan, and pour the brûlée base evenly into the ramekins. Add enough hot water to the pan to reach halfway up the sides of the ramekins. Bake for 45 minutes, or until the custard is set but still quivers in the middle. Remove the cake pan from the oven, then carefully remove the ramekins from the cake pan. Refrigerate them for at least 24 hours before serving.

When you are ready to serve, remove the ramekins from the refrigerator and allow them to stand at room temperature for 15 minutes. Sprinkle ¾ cup sugar evenly over the tops of the brûlées. Using a propane torch or a brûlée torch, melt the sugar to create a brown crust on the top of the brûlées. Let the sugar set for about 5 minutes before serving.

When a former *Dallas Morning News* columnist was asked to nominate something to put in the cornerstone of a new building, he suggested his favorite dessert, the Mansion's crème brûlée. This is Chef Bruno's interpretation. There is a layer of cooked raspberry on the bottom and it's a bit of a surprise when you bite into it. The acidity of the fruit breaks up the fat in the custard.

Lemon Pie *with crispy meringue*

YIELDS 1 (10-INCH) PIE

To make the pie dough, combine the flour and salt in a bowl. Add the butter to the flour, using your fingers to combine until the butter pieces are approximately the size of hazelnuts. Add 3 tablespoons cold water and mix with your hands until the dough comes together in a ball. Wrap the dough ball in plastic wrap, then flatten it into the shape of a disc and refrigerate for at least 2 hours.

Preheat the oven to 375 degrees F. After the dough has rested and chilled, roll the pie dough out to ⅛-inch thick. Line a 10-inch pie pan with the dough and make a fluted edge by pinching the excess dough between your thumb and forefinger and twisting slightly. Place the shell in the freezer for 20 minutes. When it is chilled, prick the bottom of the pie shell with a fork. Cover the shell with parchment paper and place dried beans or pie weights inside. Bake for 15 minutes, or until the edge of the pie crust begins to turn light brown. Remove the weights and the parchment paper, then continue baking for 10 minutes, or until the shell turns light brown on the bottom. Remove the pie shell from the oven and allow it to cool.

To make the filling, place the cornstarch, sugar, salt, zest, and 1½ cups water in a saucepan and whisk thoroughly to incorporate the ingredients. Cook the mixture over low heat until the liquid comes to a boil, stirring constantly. Boil for 2 minutes, then add the butter and continue stirring until the butter is melted. Remove the cornstarch mixture from the heat and strain to remove the zest. Place the egg yolks in a separate bowl, whisk, and add one third of the hot liquid to the egg yolks to temper. Add the egg yolks back into the cornstarch mixture, whisking to combine. Add the lemon juice and stir. Place the saucepan back over low heat and cook, stirring constantly. Bring the mixture to a boil for 1 minute, then remove the pan from the heat. Pour the mixture into the pre-baked pie shell and cover with plastic wrap in order to keep a skin from forming.

To make the topping, combine the egg whites and the cream of tartar in a mixer fitted with a whisk attachment. Beat on high speed until the whites have tripled in volume. Lower the mixer speed to medium and gradually add the sugar. Continue whipping until soft peaks form. Add the vanilla extract, return the mixer to high speed, and whip until stiff peaks form, being careful not to overwhip, which will result in a grainy meringue texture and a lot of moisture weeping on the top of the pie.

Remove the plastic cover from the filled pie shell. Using a spatula, spread the meringue into peaks and curls. Make sure that the meringue is sealed to the pie crust on all the edges, as this will keep the meringue from shrinking during baking. Place the pie on a baking sheet and bake at 375 degrees F for 10 minutes, or until the meringue has browned. Refrigerate the pie for at least 2 hours before serving to allow the filling to set.

PIE DOUGH
2 ¼ cups bread flour (may substitute all-purpose flour)
1/2 teaspoon salt
10 tablespoons unsalted butter, chilled
3 tablespoons cold water

FILLING
3 tablespoons cornstarch
1½ cups sugar
½ teaspoon salt
1 tablespoon lemon zest
6 tablespoons unsalted butter
5 egg yolks
6 tablespoons fresh lemon juice

CRISPY MERINGUE TOPPING
¾ cup egg whites, from 6 eggs
½ teaspoon cream of tartar
⅔ cup sugar
1 teaspoon vanilla extract

Source Guide

AMERICAN HOMESTEAD NATURAL MEATS
940-839-6499; homesteadnaturalmeats.com
Free-range and antibiotic-free Hampshire pork

BECKER VINEYARDS
830-644-2681; beckervineyards.com
Wines, lavender, events, bed and breakfast

BRAZOS VALLEY CHEESE
254-754-9690; brazosvalleycheese.com
Cheese

BROKEN ARROW RANCH
800-962-4263; brokenarrowranch.com
Wild game (venison, antelope, boar)

HOMESTEAD GRISTMILL
254-754-9665; homesteadgristmill.com
Stone-ground grains

TASSIONE FARMS
817-233-2751; no website
Hydroponically grown herbs and vegetables
(especially baby vegetables)

THE MOZZARELLA COMPANY
214-741-4072; mozzco.com
Mozzarella

TOM SPICER
214-954-7974; Tom Spicer's FM 1410 on Facebook
Microgreens, herbs, vegetables

Conversion Chart

All conversions are approximate.

Liquid Conversions		Weight Conversions		Oven Temperatures		
U.S.	Metric	U.S./U.K.	Metric	°F	Gas Mark	°C
1 tsp	5 ml	1/2 oz	14 g	250	1/2	120
1 tbs	15 ml	1 oz	28 g	275	1	140
2 tbs	30 ml	1 1/2 oz	43 g	300	2	150
3 tbs	45 ml	2 oz	57 g	325	3	165
1/4 cup	60 ml	2 1/2 oz	71 g	350	4	180
1/3 cup	75 ml	3 oz	85 g	375	5	190
1/3 cup + 1 tbs	90 ml	3 1/2 oz	100 g	400	6	200
1/3 cup + 2 tbs	100 ml	4 oz	113 g	425	7	220
1/2 cup	120 ml	5 oz	142 g	450	8	230
2/3 cup	150 ml	6 oz	170 g	475	9	240
3/4 cup	180 ml	7 oz	200 g	500	10	260
3/4 cup + 2 tbs	200 ml	8 oz	227 g	550	Broil	290
1 cup	240 ml	9 oz	255 g			
1 cup + 2tbs	275 ml	10 oz	284 g			
1 1/4 cups	300 ml	11 oz	312 g			
1 1/3 cups	325 ml	12 oz	340 g			
1 1/2 cups	350 ml	13 oz	368 g			
1 2/3 cups	375 ml	14 oz	400 g			
1 3/4 cups	400 ml	15 oz	425 g			
1 3/4 cups + 2 tbs	450 ml	1 lb	454 g			
2 cups (1 pint)	475 ml					
2 1/2 cups	600 ml					
3 cups	720 ml					
4 cups (1 quart)	945 ml					
	(1,000 ml is 1 liter)					